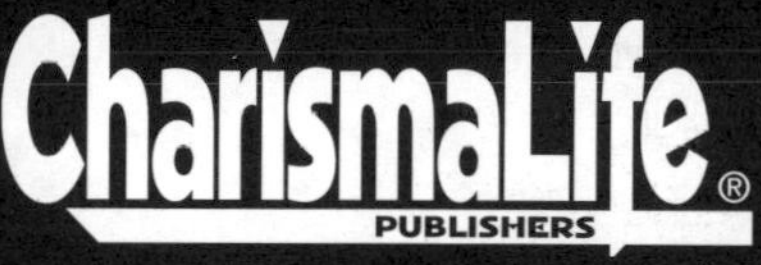

ACTS: The Church Alive!

David W. Welday III, *publisher*
Laurie Dickerson, *editor*
Rebecca Ussery, *associate editor*

Donna Winsor-Brink, Rebecca Ussery, Nancy Price, Valerie McKinney, Laurie Dickerson, Patsy Cockrum, Paul Allen, *writers*

Debbie McNab, *cover design*

ACTIVITY ZONE

Greg Cross, Kathleen Stemley, *Activity Zone artists*

Scriptures quoted from the *International Children's Bible, New Century Version,* copyright ©1986, 1988 by Word Publishing, Dallas, Texas 75039. Used by permission.

©1997 CharismaLife Publishers
600 Rinehart Road · Lake Mary, FL 32746
Editorial Offices: (407) 333-7303
Toll-Free Order Line: (800) 451-4598
ISBN 1-57405-361-2

We want to hear from you. If you have any comments, questions or suggestions, please write to the CharismaLife Editorial Department. We reserve the right to publish letters addressed to CharismaLife Publishers.

If you wish to submit new product ideas, articles or manuscripts, please write to the CharismaLife Editorial Department.

Mission Statement

Equip the body of Christ to bring children and youth into the kingdom and train them to walk and minister in the power of the Holy Spirit.

TABLE OF C

Lesson 1 — This Is Where It All Began 2
Power Point—I am part of the Church Alive!

Lesson 2 — The Church Alive Begins 14
Power Point—God and people: The real Church.

Lesson 3 — An Incredibly Exciting Day 26
Power Point—Walking with God: Never a dull moment.

Lesson 4 — Defend Your Faith! 38
Power Point—Know what you believe and believe what you know.

Lesson 5 — Are There Any Leaders in the House? 50
Power Point—Leadership: Part of God's plan for powerful ministry.

Lesson 6 — It's to Die for 62
Power Point—My choices affect many people.

Lesson 7 — Me? A Missionary? 76
Power Point—Walking with God: Risky living.

Lesson 8 — What's Your Power Source? 88
Power Point—Nothing or no one is more powerful than God.

Lesson 9 — No More Rough Edges................... 100
Power Point—Conflict: One way to grow.

Lesson 10 — Heavenly Hearing Aids 112
Power Point—Not hard of hearing—hard at hearing.

Lesson 11 — Spread It Around 124
Power Point—My mission: Anyone, anyplace.

Lesson 12 — Suffering for Jesus 136
Power Point—God and I: Ultimate victors.

Lesson 13 — It Never Ends 148
Power Point—Acts: The never-ending story.

SPECIAL PAGES

A Letter From the Editor 37
Components of *Club 56* 75
Power Points... 123
Recipes... 159
Memory Verses.. 160
Activities Chart.. 159

ITEMS NEEDED FOR LESSON

❑ Dry erase boards (two)
❑ Markers (two)

1—Game

❑ Notebook paper
❑ Pencils
❑ Prize (small)

2—Bible Study

❑ *Club 56 Activity Zone* page 1
❑ Bibles
❑ Pencils

❑ Bibles
❑ Chalkboard
❑ Chalk
❑ Newspapers
❑ Masking tape

3—Music

❑ Cassette recorder
❑ Cassette (blank)

4—Problem Solving

❑ *Club 56 Activity Zone* page 2

❑ Bibles
❑ Paper (card stock)
❑ Scissors
❑ Markers
❑ Tape (double-stick)

❑ Copies of *Club 56 Leader's Manual* cover sheet page 37
❑ Copies of *Club 56 Leader's Manual* Lesson 1 ACTS File Page page 13
❑ File folders
❑ Markers
❑ Glue
❑ Scissors

❑ None

SPECIAL NOTE

You will be offering students a prayer time for the baptism in the Holy Spirit. As you prepare this week, ask the Lord to set up that time in His way, give you wisdom for the prayer time and plant the seed of desire in the students' hearts.

There is a helpful, child-friendly tract called "New Kid in the Spirit" available through CharismaLife Publishers. This 8-page booklet helps children understand what the baptism in the Spirit is and how to receive it. Call 1-800-451-4598 to order.

I am part of the Church Alive!

But the Holy Spirit will come to you. Then you will receive power. You will be my witnesses—in Jerusalem, in all of Judea, in Samaria, and in every part of the world.

Acts 1:8

Acts 1:1-26

A. Get a Life!

B. Pass It On

C. Ready, Set, Go for It!

THIS IS WHERE IT ALL BEGAN

It happened again. Josh came home with another story of how his sociology teacher said the Church was a place for weak and needy people to socialize and try to solve their problems. He was discouraged that he and other Christians in his class tried to stand up for their faith but were constantly shot down because of their teacher's "educated outlook on life." Everything they said seemed to bring ridicule and sarcasm from their teacher because they sounded "stupid."

As we discussed it at the dinner table, I finally asked Josh if he had prayed and asked God to give him wisdom as to how he should speak to this teacher. We joined together and asked God what to do with the situation. As we prayed, my youngest asked the Holy Spirit to be in the classroom with her brother so he could say the right thing that would cause his teacher to see the love of God.

In a few days Josh came home excited about what had happened in class that day. Again, his teacher had been talking about the Church and how sad it was. Josh asked the Holy Spirit to help him show God's love to the teacher. It was awesome! Different students in the class began to say things regarding comments he had made about the Church and the Lord began turning each of his statements around to positive ones. The entire class agreed that the purpose of the Church was to be a place of help, encouragement and hope, and that our society needed that today.

What an encouragement to Josh to see that God still works through His people today. The Church is alive, and God wants to use it to touch people throughout our communities through each one of us who is willing to let Him be what He needs to be through us.

Materials: Dry erase boards (two) and markers (two).

Before class: Write "The Church Alive" on the top of one whiteboard and "The Church Almost Dead" on the top of the other.

Today we begin a new series of lessons on the book of Acts. Tell me the first five books of the New Testament. *Matthew, Mark, Luke, John and Acts.* The first four of those books are called "The Gospels." They talk about the life, actions, death and resurrection of Jesus Christ. Acts, the next book, tells about the actions of the disciples after Jesus' resurrection.

The subtitle of the quarter's lessons tells us that Acts is about the Church Alive! Each week you will see how the early Church was really alive and how we are to be the Church Alive.

Divide students into two groups, the Church Alive and the Church Almost Dead. Give each team its board and marker. Neither team should be able to see the other's board.

You and your team have three minutes to write as many ideas as you can on your whiteboard that would illustrate what is written on the top. Think about things we do in church, who we are as the Church, things we do with God, etc. How would the Church Alive look doing that? What about the Church Almost Dead? Use the following things or think of your own: worship, pastoring children, pastors preaching, sick people getting healed.

At the end of three minutes, have each team pantomime two of their ideas for the other team. The other team should guess what they are portraying.

Let's find out how we can be the Church Alive!

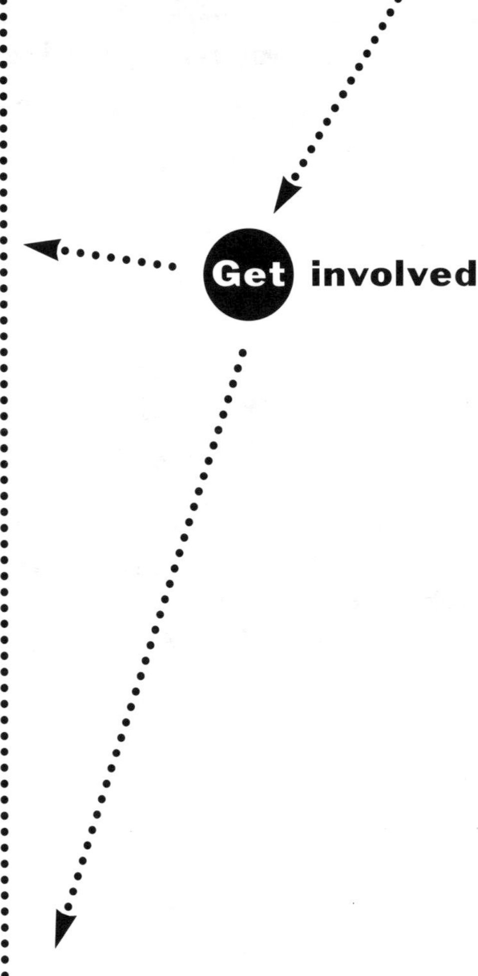

Materials: Bibles, chalkboard, chalk, newspapers and masking tape.

Before class: Make two batons by wrapping two sections of the newspapers into cylindrical shapes and taping them to stay that way.

Get a Life!

How many of you keep journals or diaries? Have you ever gone back and read what you wrote down a year or two earlier? *(Allow students time to*

I am part of the Church Alive!

Pray that God will renew your vision as to how you can encourage your local church to be the Church Alive! Are there things that have come into your life that keep the Holy Spirit from doing a mighty work in your ministry with the gifts He has given you?

share.) Luke, a doctor who believed Jesus was the Messiah, kept a diary of Jesus' ministry. It is written for us in the book named "Luke" in our Bibles. Now that Jesus had died and was resurrected, it was time for Luke to write another book. It was time to write about the things God was doing by His Spirit through the apostles. The name of this book is Acts. We will be studying the book of Acts for the next several weeks.

Why do you think the Holy Spirit encouraged Luke to call this book "Acts?" *It records the acts or actions of the disciples and the Holy Spirit.* This book tells about Jesus' followers receiving power to do the things Jesus did (plus more!) through the Holy Spirit.

Let's look at how the book starts. *(Have a student read Acts 1:1-5.)*

Jesus encouraged His disciples that not only would they see what He had done during His ministry time on earth, but also that the same ministry was able to happen by the Holy Spirit through each of them.

How many of you would like to see God do miracles through your life? In order to see these miracles, we also have to follow what Jesus told the disciples: We must wait for the baptism in the Holy Spirit.

Jesus told the disciples they could be full of the Holy Spirit, full of God Himself. The rest of the accounts in Acts happened because the disciples were baptized in and full of the Holy Spirit. Jesus told the disciples to wait until they had experienced this baptism before they became witnesses for Him.

How many of you have been baptized in the Holy Spirit? *(Have students share their experiences of being baptized in the Spirit. Share your own.)* At the end of our Bible Lesson today, I will give you an opportunity to receive the baptism in the Holy Spirit if you have not yet done so.

Pass It On

In a relay race in the Olympics, the runners carry a baton. **What happens to the baton during the race?** *It is passed from each runner to the next runner on his team.*

As you can see, I have two batons here. I would like you to split yourselves into two even teams. *(Allow students to do so. Each team should stand in a line facing the front. They should space themselves by putting their right arms on the shoulders of the persons in front of them.)* Now you are ready to be baton-passers. We're not going to run today. We're only practicing passing the baton. To pass it to the next person, you must hold one end and they must grab the other. When you are both holding it, the first person lets go. Go ahead and try it once before we do a relay. *(Allow time for this.)*

Now, let's have a race. Ready, set, go! *(Be sure the teams follow the directions to have the passer and the receiver both holding the baton before the passer releases it to the receiver. Declare a winner.)* You were great at that. Now, let's try it with some twists. *(Continue with the relays, using one of these ideas for each race: the passer and receiver may not look at each other; the passer and receiver must use their left hands to pass; the baton has to go under the passer's legs to the receiver. When the relays are done, have students make observations about when and why the baton was dropped during the relays.)*

The most crucial part of a relay race is the passing of the baton to the next person. They both have to be running the same speed, one in front of the other. They have to be very careful in giving and receiving the baton. They can lose momentum in the race if the baton is dropped and one runner has to pick it up, just like what happened in our races.

Let's look at what happened when Jesus "passed the baton" to His disciples. *(Read Acts 1:6-11.)* The disciples were to carry the baton and then pass it on to the next generation of Christians. It has continued to be passed on, even to your generation. Did you know it is your responsibility to "pass the baton" on to the generation that follows yours?

♦ Who are some people who have passed the baton on to you?

♦ What do you think it means to "pass the baton"? *Telling others of Christ; showing God's love; participating in God's miracles; etc.*

♦ What is one way you could pass the baton to the next generation? *Telling younger kids about Jesus; telling kids your own age about what Jesus means to you; etc.*

If Jesus' talking to them and passing on the baton was not enough to blow the disciples away, an incredible thing happened next. All of a sudden, Jesus was lifted up into heaven. Remember, this was before *Star Trek* and "Beam me up, Scotty" were even thought of. It was way before any of our modern technology. Imagine seeing Jesus suddenly going up into the sky. *(Have students stop and think about what it must have been like.)* To top off this unusual disappearing act, as the disciples stood there looking up at Jesus leaving, two beings appeared and asked them what they were doing. The angels didn't seem all that surprised. In fact, they went on to tell the disciples that Jesus would come back the same way He left—in the clouds!

Ready, Set, Go for It!

(Read Acts 1:12-15,21-26.) The disciples went back to Jerusalem after they regained their composure. They went to a meeting place in an upstairs room. People came in and out. They prayed. They talked about what had happened to Judas. They decided the time had come to replace Judas with another person.

♦ Whom did they find? *Matthias and Joseph Barsabbas.*

♦ What made Matthias and Joseph Barsabbas good candidates? *They were with the group when Jesus was in human form, from the beginning to the end of His ministry.*

Today, there is no human alive who witnessed the baptism or resurrection of Jesus Christ. **How can we still be witnesses and disciples of His? What would the qualifications be today?** *(Have students get into groups of three or four and come up with two qualifications for a disciple today. Have each group share, and write their answers on the chalkboard.) Someone who spends time with Jesus; obeys God; knows how God thinks because he has read His Word; listens to Him; etc.*

Disciples of Jesus are people who spend time with Him. They read God's Word because they want to know how to live. They follow His directions.

I am part of the Church Alive!

Having students see the disciples' human sides helps them to understand that they didn't have any "super-spiritual" life. They were people just like we are who were willing for the Holy Spirit to use them in a supernatural way.

Don't use examples just from Scripture about how God is alive in His people. Use examples of how He has used you supernaturally.

"New Kid in the Spirit," a tract to help kids understand and receive the baptism in the Holy Spirit, is available from CharismaLife by calling 1-800-451-4598.

Acts 1:8

But the Holy Spirit will come to you. Then you will receive power. You will be my witnesses—in Jerusalem, in all of Judea, in Samaria, and in every part of the world.

♦ Who are some people you know who meet these qualifications?

♦ Do you meet the qualifications we have just given of a disciple? If not, how could you?

Conclusion

For the next 12 weeks, we will be learning about events in the book of Acts. Acts shows people who are being the Church Alive. It shows the beginning of the Church.

Now it's our turn. We can also be the Church Alive right now in the 1990s. The Church Alive isn't just about adults. It's also about 5th and 6th graders like you being the Church Alive in your families, at your schools and with your relatives and friends. We're going to pray in just a minute. If you want to be part of the Church Alive this week, be sure to ask the Lord for His help when we pray.

If you have not yet received the baptism in the Holy Spirit, this is a great time to ask for that. Remember, the people who were part of the first church that began in the book of Acts had to wait until they were baptized in the Holy Spirit before they began the ministry God was calling them to.

Lord Jesus, we want to be the Church Alive. We don't want to just come to Sunday School, pray sometimes and maybe read the Bible occasionally. We really want to be Your Church, alive in our world. Please help us this week to spend time with You, listen and obey Your instructions and watch the wonderful things You will do through us. Jesus, some of us haven't yet been baptized in Your Holy Spirit. We pray this morning that You would baptize each one of those. We want to have Your power working through us, and the only way for that to happen is for us to be full of Your Holy Spirit. In Jesus' name, amen.

(Have students who want the baptism in the Holy Spirit come and pray with you in a group. Lay hands on each, asking Jesus to baptize him. After praying, ask each one what he experienced.)

Materials: Bibles, paper (card stock), scissors, markers and tape (double-stick).

Before class: Cut paper into 1/2- by 3-inch strips. Each student will need nine strips.

Note: Card stock can often be purchased at greatly reduced prices from a print shop's overstock supply. It comes in many different colors.

Look in Acts 1:8. Have a student read the Memory Verse. **This is our Memory Verse today.** It is an inspiring promise from Jesus. He promised

---

the Holy Spirit and power so we can be witnesses everywhere we go. Today we will make a mini-verse chain to help us remember we are witnesses and that we are linked to the disciples in the early Church by the Holy Spirit's work in us.

Instruct your class to write one phrase per strip. Have them write Acts 1:8 on two strips of paper, one for the beginning of their chains and one for the end. Phrases are:

◊ Acts 1:8
◊ But the Holy Spirit
◊ will come to you.
◊ Then you will receive power.
◊ You will be my witnesses—
◊ in Jerusalem,
◊ in all of Judea, in Samaria,
◊ and in every part of the world.
◊ Acts 1:8

Students should use the tape to make the strips into links, attaching one link to the next by slipping the new paper through the already-taped link, taping the new paper to itself to make another link. Words should face out.

Think of a place for your mini-verse chain, a place where you will see it several times this week. Have students give ideas such as on their bikes' handlebars, hanging from mirrors, attached to the headboards of their beds, etc. **Whenever you see it, try to say it without looking. If you can't remember, look at the words. Let it be a reminder to you to receive the Holy Spirit's power and be His witnesses this week. Remember, you are the Church Alive!**

1—Game

Materials: Notebook paper, pencils and prize (small).

Our Memory Verse tells us we will be witnesses of God to others as we are filled with the Holy Spirit and God's power. Being a good witness means being able to tell about or demonstrate what we have seen or experienced. Let's see what good witnesses you are. Find a partner. Turn your chairs so you and your partner are sitting back-to-back.

Hand out notebook paper and pencils. **Your assignment is to write, in as much detail as you can, what your partner is wearing. No peeking! You have one minute to write as much as you can. Go.**

When they have completed the minute, have them turn around and compare what they wrote with what they see. **How did you do?** Have students respond.

When doing this activity, think of and share examples from your church of how God has used someone in each of the areas listed.

Activity Zone page 1

Activity Zone page 1 Answers

Galatians 2:10—Help the poor.

Galatians 5:13—Serve each other.

Luke 18:1—Pray and don't lose hope.

Psalm 95:6—Worship God.

1 Corinthians 14:31—Prophesy (speak God's words to each other)

Ephesians 4:15-16—Speak the truth with love. Grow up to be like Christ. Depend on Christ. Do your own part in the body of Christ.

Stand in the front of the room. **Turn your chairs around so you are facing the back wall.** Students should be facing away from you. **Write down these things, as I ask for them. Don't turn your heads this way. I want to see which of you are witnesses of what you've seen today.**

♦ What is the color of my eyes?

♦ How many rings do I have on my fingers?

♦ What is written on the chalkboard?

♦ How many doors are in the front wall of our classroom?

♦ What picture (or poster) is hanging on the wall behind me?

♦ What kind and color of clothes do I have on?

♦ What does my hair look like today? Include things like what side it's parted on, what is in my hair, is it short or long, etc.

Have students turn around. Give the prize to the person who wrote down the most details.

You all are witnesses to things every day. A part of being the Church Alive is spending time with the Lord and being witnesses of Him and His work in your life, just as the disciples were witnesses.

2—Bible Study

Materials: *Club 56 Activity Zone* page 1, Bibles and pencils.

Give students their *Activity Zone* pages. **We talk about "the Church" all the time. We hear about it at church, from our parents, in the news and from our friends. But what is the purpose of the Church? If someone were to have you describe the Church, what would you say? Write down at least three statements that describe the Church.** Have students do this before moving on to the next part of the *Activity Zone* page.

Now read Hebrews 10:25 on the page. It says the Church is a place where we should come together and meet to encourage one another. Encouragement comes in many different forms. Let's look up a few Scriptures and write down how we can be an encouragement to one another in the church.

Remember, the Church is not just the building we meet in! The Church is God's people who have come together to worship Him and encourage each other in Jesus. The Church is alive! The only thing that will keep it alive and well is for us to be willing to be "God in the flesh" for other people to see.

3—Music

Materials: Cassette recorder and cassette (blank).

Before class: Record some of the theme songs from popular television shows or movies. Record only about 20 seconds of each of the songs. Some suggestions of shows you might want to record are: "Home Improvement," "Sesame Street," *Star Wars, The Lion King, Mission Impossible* or Saturday morning cartoon shows.

Theme songs are very important to the success of TV shows and movies. The songs that are played at the beginning set you up for the show to come. For example, if the song sounded mysterious and threatening, what kind of show would you expect to see?

Theme songs become so closely identified with their show that people can remember the words and the tune years later. I am going to test you by playing some popular theme songs. See if you can guess what movie or TV show they are from.

Play the recordings. Stop after each segment and give the students a chance to guess what show or movie it is from. Chances are the students will recognize them quickly.

- ♦ How did the music help set up the show?
- ♦ How do the words of the songs help you to know more about the show?

The book of Acts tells us about the beginning of the Church.

- ♦ If you were given the assignment of writing a theme song to introduce the new Church Alive, what kind of song would you write?

- ♦ Would it be fast or slow?

- ♦ Would you make it instrumental or would it have lyrics?

- ♦ What kind of style would you make it?

- ♦ Do you think a catchy theme song would have helped with the popularity of the early Church?

Allow for some discussion time as the students brainstorm and figure out what kind of a song would best represent and introduce the Church.

4—Problem Solving

Materials: *Club 56 Activity Zone* page 2.

When we read in Scripture different things that happened to Jesus' disciples, sometimes we forget that these men were human beings just like we are. They had many of the same questions and feelings that we have today. I think that sometimes they wondered if they were doing the right thing. Let's look at this *Activity Zone* page and think about what it would have been like if they had done something different from what we know they did do.

Have students talk about what they think would have happened in each case. Allow them to be creative. For instance, if they had left Jerusalem, where might the disciples have gone? What sight-seeing might have been done? How might the Lord have led them back to His purpose in sending the Holy Spirit?

I am part of the Church Alive!

Activity Zone page 2

Help your class realize their importance to your church. The adults who are in authority now will not always be there. God may be raising up someone in your class to take an important role in the church.

I am part of the Church Alive!

Keilani watched as her older sister packed her suitcase. "You're going to have a lot of fun, Anji!" said Keilani.

"This is a mission, Keilani," answered Anji. "We're going to help build a church building in 105° weather. I don't think anyone would call that fun!"

Keilani laughed, "I mean you'll have fun with all the kids who are going. I wish I could go! I don't think it's fair that you have to be in high school to go on this trip. Everyone gets to do something for God except me."

Anji stopped packing for a minute and sat down. "Keilani, do you remember when your friend Lisa was very sad? Her parents were fighting a lot and she felt alone and afraid? You told her that Jesus would love to be her friend and Savior. She asked you how to become a Christian. That, little sister, was doing something for God. You were being a witness for Him."

Keilani thought for a minute as her sister returned to her packing. "You know that song that says, 'I'm the Church and you're the Church' if we are Christians?" asked Keilani. "I wonder how old you have to be to really **be** the Church?" Anji put a shirt into the suitcase, smiled and put out her hand. "Keilani Evans, congratulations. You are the Church! Now go be the Church in your own room, OK?"

Keilani walked out of Anji's room and went to the kitchen to find her mother.

"Mom, when do I get to do a fun thing like the mission trip Anji is doing? Does God have age requirements?"

Her mother laughed. "Keilani, just be ready to tell people what you know about Jesus and you can make your own mission trip every day. I have a very important ministry for you right now. How about going over to help Mrs. Maxwell with the twins for a while this afternoon?"

Keilani grimaced, "Mom, they're terrors! How can I tell Mrs. Maxwell about Jesus when her brats are screaming their heads off? No, I want something more interesting like Anji is doing!"

Her mother turned from the stove and looked at Keilani. "Which is more important: helping Mrs. Maxwell or building a church?"

Keilani wasn't sure.

What do you think?

Divide the class into two groups. Assign each group one of the two positions to defend. (The two positions are: building a church and helping Mrs. Maxwell.) Have the students consider these questions before they begin their discussion.

♦ What seemed to be the most appealing part of Anji's trip to Keilani?

- ♦ When do children become a "real" part of the Church?

- ♦ How can 5th and 6th graders have important responsibilities in the Church?

- ♦ How can a 5th or 6th grader know what is important to God?

I am part of the Church Alive!

Materials: Copies of *Club 56 Leader's Manual* cover sheet page 37 (bottom half of page), copies of *Club 56 Leader's Manual* Lesson 1 ACTS File Page page 13, file folders, markers, glue and scissors.

Over the next several weeks, our class will be acting as consultants for a major computer company hired to help churches become more like the church in Acts. The name of the company you will be working for is "Alive Church Technology Services" or "ACTS." You will be compiling one report a week through interviews, observations and research.

Have students create a folder for their upcoming Challenges. Give each student a folder and cover sheet. Encourage group members to color the ACTS cover sheets and glue them to the front of their folders. Students may choose to use all of the cover sheet or portions they cut out.

Your Challenge for the ACTS company this week is to ask friends, members of your family and people in your church to tell you what one thing they like the most about church. ACTS is trying to find the perfect Church Alive service.

Read the list from the screen to each person you ask. Tally the responses you collect.

Then create a two-hour church service schedule based on your findings. Decide the length of each portion of the service. For example, if "Announcements" gets the most responses, the announcement portion of the service should be the longest. Write your church service schedule on the computer screen.

Each week you will need to remember to bring these File Pages back so we can put them in your folders. What do you think will help you remember them? Have students give ideas. Follow up with any that involve you, such as phoning the kids on Saturday to remind them, etc.

Parts of a Worship Service

Worship

Preaching

Special Music

Ministry

Offering

Communion

Socializing

Testimonies

Announcements

Skits

Alive Church Technology Services

Ask friends, members of your family and people in your church to tell you what one thing they like the most about church. Tally the responses you collect. Next, use the answers to create a two-hour church service schedule. Based on your findings, decide the length of each portion of the service, using the list on the screen. For example, if "Announcements" gets the most answers, the announcements portion of the service should be the longest.

ITEMS NEEDED FOR LESSON

❏ ACTS folders
❏ Lesson 1 ACTS File Pages

1—Drama

❏ *Club 56 Activity Zone* page 3
❏ Bible (large family-size)
❏ Pencils

2—Object Lesson

❏ Chalkboard
❏ Chalk
❏ Pictures of some of the great churches of the world
❏ Paper
❏ Pencils

❏ Paper bag
❏ Unusual objects
❏ Blindfold

❏ Bibles
❏ Chalkboard
❏ Chalk

3—Game

❏ *Club 56 Activity Zone* page 4
❏ Dice (three, or spinners with numbers)
❏ Prizes (three, small)

❏ Bibles
❏ Chalkboard
❏ Chalk
❏ Plaster of Paris
❏ Clay (or play dough)
❏ Food coloring
❏ Wax paper
❏ Spoon
❏ Bowl (large, disposable)
❏ Knives (plastic)

4—Outreach Project

❏ Pencils
❏ Papers
❏ Envelopes

❏ None

❏ Copies of *Club 56 Leader's Manual* Lesson 2 ACTS File Page page 25

SPECIAL NOTE

For More Activities 2 you will need pictures of great churches of the world. These can be obtained through your local library, the Internet, your pastor(s) or encyclopedias (either books or computer files).

For the Memory Verse Activity, you will need clay or play dough. A recipe for play dough is on *Club 56 Leader's Manual* page 159.

God and people: The real Church

They spent their time learning the apostles' teaching. And they continued to share, to break bread, and to pray together.

Acts 2:42

Acts 2

A. Look Up

B. Look Out

C. Look Around

THE CHURCH ALIVE BEGINS

What is the Church? I was reminded dramatically two years ago that the Church is more than just buildings and institutions, or even just the group of people with whom you fellowship.

That was when I was diagnosed with a neuromuscular disease that had taken over my body. I was faced with the decision to have surgery, which might or might not help.

How could this be happening to me? I was relatively young (40 years old), had a wonderful wife, four great kids and a secure position in ministry in a large church. My life was too busy to have to deal with something like this. Yet life as I knew it came to a complete halt. The only thing that was important was taking care of this disease and getting well.

That's when my church stepped in. Different people began taking parts of my responsibilities at the church. Others provided child care and helped with our children. Still others gave my wife the necessary physical and emotional help. And they all prayed for a positive outcome from my surgery, as well as a good prognosis. The Holy Spirit let us see Him working through others to touch our lives.

Through God's wisdom and provision, my surgery went well and recovery was quick. Through the church's graciousness and interaction with our family, we were able to keep up with all the regular home and family duties.

Today I still have the disease, but His grace is sufficient. I learned a vital lesson through the whole experience—the church I attend really is a part of the Church Alive! He used His church to reach out to us, and I am so thankful for Him and for them.

challenge review

Materials: ACTS folders and Lesson 1 ACTS File Pages.

Your Challenge for the Alive Church Technology Service this week was to ask people to tell you what one thing they like most about church. On the File Page you took home, you should have tallied their responses and set up a church service schedule based on your findings.

Have students share their church service schedules.

♦ How were the results similar to what you expected? How were they different?

♦ What is your favorite part of church?

♦ How would your schedule look if you were planning a church service?

Have students put their Lesson 1 ACTS File Pages into their ACTS folders.

opening activity

Materials: Paper bag, unusual objects and blindfold.

Note: The unusual objects should be ones that would be unusual to a 5th or 6th grader, or unusual because they are out of place in your classroom. Here are some ideas for unusual objects: pincushion, piece of cheesecloth, bolt, bungee cord, hairpiece, hackysack, milk jug lid, etc.

Have you ever been taken totally off guard by something? Share with your class an event that surprised you. Let them share one that surprised them.

I have several objects in this bag. I will ask one person at a time to wear the blindfold, put his hand in the bag and try to guess what one object is. I will tell you that the things in this sack are not your usual, run-of-the-mill items. When you touch an item, feel it all over and tell us what you think it is and what it might be used for.

Let a different person play each time. Have the student take the object out of the bag and tell what the object is and what its function is. If she cannot guess what the object is, give her a clue.

Those were unusual, weren't they? In our lesson today we are going to see how one day God surprised His followers in an unusual way with something they were expecting—the Holy Spirit. Let's get right into the lesson and see how awesome God was on that day!

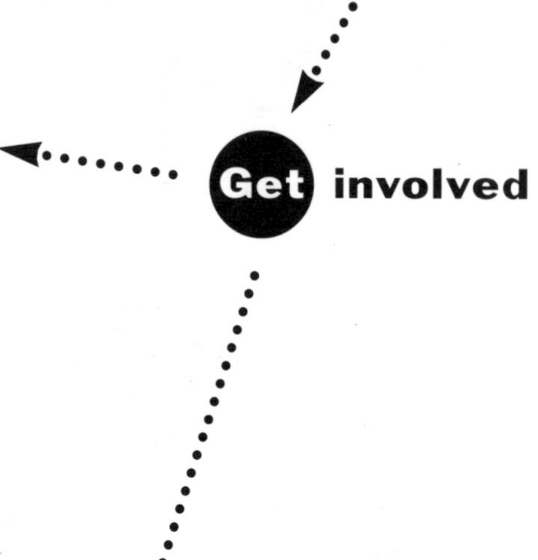

Lord, use this lesson to touch the lives of my kids, who will in turn touch the lives of those around them so that Your Church will be used mightily in both our community and the world. Amen.

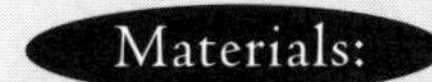
Materials: Bibles, chalkboard and chalk.

Look Up

Have you ever been expecting a surprise but weren't sure when it was going to happen? *(Have kids share stories. Share one yourself.)* Even though you think you're prepared, the waiting can be both exciting and frustrating. The followers of Christ who were waiting for the Holy Spirit must have been feeling the same sort of things when they were waiting for the promised Holy Spirit. Jesus had told them to wait. Every day must have been full of great anticipation and perhaps disappointment when the gift didn't appear that day. The day He was sent finally did come, though, and the disciples were blown away by what God did. Let's look at what happened.

(Have a student read Acts 2:1-4.) The Holy Spirit made quite an entrance, didn't He? God sent His gift with unusual sights and sounds: a strong wind, flames of fire over each person's head and people speaking in other languages. Let's see the responses of some religious Jews who overheard what happened. *(Read Acts 2:5-13.)*

♦ **How do you think the disciples reacted to this event?** *Overjoyed and filled with excitement at what God had promised.*

♦ **How did the religious Jews respond?** *They were amazed and confused. Some made fun of the disciples.*

♦ **How do you think you would have responded to what happened if you were a disciple? If you were a visitor to Jerusalem?**

Last week we talked about the baptism in the Holy Spirit. *(Review by reading through the Conclusion of the Bible Lesson in Lesson 1.)* The disciples had to wait for this gift before launching out in God's ministry. Now we see that the gift was given, and He made quite a stir.

♦ **What was the purpose of the Holy Spirit's coming?** *To have God live inside His people.*

♦ **What is the purpose of the Holy Spirit in your life?** *To have God living inside you!*

When the Holy Spirit is living in you, He will change your life and the lives of people around you, just as He did with the disciples. Let's see what happened after they were baptized in the Holy Spirit.

Look Out

There were a lot of things happening all at once. **What were they?** *People understood the disciples in their own languages. The religious Jews made fun of the disciples. Many were amazed at what they saw and heard. The scene was probably on the verge of becoming quite chaotic when Peter stood up with the 11 and got everyone's attention.*

God and people: The real Church.

First, he explained that they were not drunk because it was only 9 o'clock in the morning. Then Peter began speaking to the crowd in a way they would understand. He used Scripture from Joel and Psalms to show God's truth regarding what happened. Listen to what he said. *(Read Acts 2:17-21,25-28,31,34-35.)*

What a wonderful message he gave to the people! Not only did the Holy Spirit use this opportunity to show His power, but He also used it to show God's love for the people, who a short time earlier, crucified Christ in their desire to see an end to His ministry.

Look at Peter's message to the people to see how the Holy Spirit was preparing the hearts of the people to turn to Christ. *(Have someone read Acts 2:22-24,33)* Peter gave a clear presentation of the good news, and the Holy Spirit used his message to bring the people to Christ. Look back at your Bibles and tell me what the important parts of the message were. This will give us a better understanding of why the people were "sick at heart" because of what they heard. *(Write the following verse numbers on the board. Have students tell what they think is important from each one.)*

◊ **Verse 22**—*Jesus did miracles, wonders and signs.*

◊ **Verse 23**—*He was nailed to the cross.*

◊ **Verse 24**—*God raised Jesus from death.*

◊ **Verse 33**—*Jesus is at God's right side and has given us the Holy Spirit.*

◊ **Verse 36**—*God has made Jesus both Lord and Christ. The people were responsible for nailing Him to the cross.*

The people were sick at heart when Peter told them that they had crucified God's Son. They realized they were sinners, yet heard Peter express how much God still loved them. In verse 37 they asked Peter what they should do. Having been a fisherman, Peter knew just when to draw in the net to catch a heavy load. He told them they must change their hearts and lives and be baptized in the name of Jesus Christ for the forgiveness of their sins. Not only would God forgive them, but also He would give them the gift of the Holy Spirit.

About 3,000 people were added to the Church that day! **Can you imagine 3,000 people being added to our church today? Where would they sit? Who would baptize them all?** *(Allow students time to think through what having 3,000 new members would mean to your church. A healthy church is usually 1/4 to 1/3 kids up to 6th grade. This means 750-1,000 kids added to the Sunday School. Where would they sit? Who would teach them?)* Those 3,000 were not added to one congregation at a particular church building, but to God's Church, the Church Alive.

Look Around

The last few verses of Acts 2 are perhaps some of the most descriptive words of what the function of the church should be. The functions are the same for our church today. The Church Alive will be exhibiting these characteristics until Christ's return.

Notice Peter's words were orchestrated by the Holy Spirit. Before any of your lessons, ask Him to speak His words through you to those listening. He always knows what both the speaker and the listener need to hear.

Now is a good time to ask your class if they understand what Peter taught. Be sensitive to kids who have not yet received Christ as their personal Savior. Allow the Holy Spirit to guide you.

God and people: The real Church.

♦ **In verse 42, what four things did they do?** *They learned the apostles' teachings, shared with each other, ate in each other's homes and prayed together.*

♦ **What is one characteristic of the people that occurs three times in verses 42-46?** *(Have students individually look at those verses.) They shared.*

♦ **What things does it say they shared?** *Everything, their food.*

♦ **Why is it important for 5th and 6th grade Christians to share with other Christians? How could you do that?**

(Point out to the students how your church fulfills the four characteristics of a Church Alive. For instance: listening to and learning from the pastor and other leaders; getting together in home groups to fellowship; eating together and praying for each other. Be specific so kids see that your church is functioning this way.)

Let's talk about our class as a church. We can demonstrate the characteristics of the Church whenever we see each other. **How can we do the four things that are mentioned in Acts?** *(Explore with the class how your Club 56 can be like the early Church in these four ways. Let kids give ideas. Plan ways to implement the ideas given.)*

Those were good ideas on how we can be the Church Alive! Our Power Point today is ***God and people: The real Church.*** The Church is not a building or buildings. It's not this room we meet in. The Church is **people.** It's you and God, me and *(point to and name each person in Club 56)* and God together.

Conclusion

What a wonderful time in Church history! The last verse of Acts 2 tells us that they praised God and all the people liked them. More and more people were added to the Church every day because of the Holy Spirit's moving in the lives of the earliest believers. How exciting!

The same Father, Son and Holy Spirit are still working in the Church today. We can experience what the earliest believers experienced if we want to. The Holy Spirit came to bring people to a place of turning from their sin and turning to Christ. He came to empower His people so they could do His work. The Holy Spirit is still doing the same work today through His people.

Everything else we hear and learn about in the book of Acts is dependent on this one act—the giving of the gift of the Holy Spirit.

The same is true in your life. Everything you do for God is dependent on your receiving and walking in the gift of the Holy Spirit—God living in you.

(Pray with your class concerning receiving Christ, receiving the baptism in the Holy Spirit or recommitting their lives to Christ. Be confident in praying with them regarding these decisions. Remind students that it's God who does the work. Their job is to be the vessels who are willing to let Him do His work through them.)

Understanding the work of the Holy Spirit in your own life is important before you can help your class to understand. Ask the Holy Spirit to do a fresh work in your life as you minister to your class.

Materials: Bibles, chalkboard, chalk, Plaster of Paris, clay (or play dough), food coloring, wax paper, bowl (large, disposable), spoon and knives (plastic).

Before class: On chalkboard, make four columns with these four titles: Teaching, Sharing, Breaking Bread and Praying.

Note: A recipe for play dough can be found on page 159.

Our Memory Verse tells us that Jesus' followers spent their time learning the apostles' teaching, sharing, breaking bread and praying. We are going to take a few minutes to learn the verse, and then we are going to use the verse to make a group project.

Give students a few minutes to use their Bibles to look up and memorize the verse.

Divide the class into four groups. Assign each group one of the four titles to work with. **We are going to make plaster molds that represent the four ways that Jesus' followers spent their time.**

Give each student a sheet of wax paper and a mound of clay about the size of a golf ball. Instruct the students to work with the clay until it becomes soft enough to flatten into a small pancake on top of the wax paper.

Now that you have your clay pancake, you are going to carve a symbol or words that represent your group's title. Let's think of some ideas you could use.

Brainstorm with the class for ideas to carve in the clay, such as a Bible or ear for teaching, a mouth for sharing, bread for breaking bread and hands for praying. With the plastic knives, the students should make the impressions deep into the clay without tearing the bottom.

While the students are working, mix up the plaster by adding one part water and two parts plaster in a large bowl. More plaster can be added to reduce the hardening time. Stir in food coloring.

After the students have carved their clay, scoop a heaping spoonful of plaster onto it. Have the students use the plastic knives to spread the plaster so it covers the entire impression. Allow the plaster to harden (about ten minutes) while you lead another activity. When the plaster has hardened, peel off the clay.

The students will then have hard casts of their designs. Have them put their plaster design in the tray of the chalkboard under the word their group was assigned. Have each person tell why she selected the symbol she did.

Acts 2:42

They spent their time learning the apostles' teaching. And they continued to share, to break bread, and to pray together.

God and people: The real Church.

Activity Zone page 3

1—Drama

Materials: *Club 56 Activity Zone* page 3, Bible (large family-size) and pencils.

Divide class into groups of three. Give each member of the groups her *Activity Zone* page. Have groups follow the directions. Give the groups ten minutes to fill in the blanks and practice the skit. Have each group perform their skit for the rest of the class.

2—Object Lesson

Materials: Chalkboard, chalk, pictures of some of the great churches of the world, paper and pencils.

Before class: Print these options on the chalkboard:

- ◊ Simple, small sanctuary—$50,000
- ◊ More elaborate, medium-sized sanctuary—$100,000
- ◊ Ornate, large sanctuary—$200,000
- ◊ Classrooms—$10,000 each
- ◊ Bathrooms—$15,000 each
- ◊ Fellowship hall—$10,000 (extra $5,000 to include tables and chairs)
- ◊ Kitchen—$25,000
- ◊ Office space—$10,000 per office (must have at least three offices)
- ◊ Gym—$20,000
- ◊ Paved parking lot—$25,000
- ◊ Brick exterior—$20,000
- ◊ Wood exterior—$10,000
- ◊ Natural stone exterior—$25,000
- ◊ Stained glass window—$10,000
- ◊ Bell tower—$25,000
- ◊ Landscaping—$25,000
- ◊ Pipe organ—$25,000

Let's look at some pictures I have brought with me. These are some examples of some of the greatest churches and cathedrals that have ever been built. As you show the pictures, tell the students some of the facts or details about each building.

- ♦ What do you think of these?
- ♦ Would you like to go to church in any of these?
- ♦ Which one would you like to attend?

Now let's review our Power Point for today. *God and people: The real Church.*

Are you confused? If the real church is made up of us (people), why has man spent so much money, time and effort into building such grand cathedrals?

♦ Do you think it is wrong to build such huge church buildings?

♦ What might be some of the right or wrong reasons for building a grand church building?

♦ What kind of church would you want to build? Why?

Though people, for many different reasons, have felt the need to build elaborate buildings to worship in, the Bible reminds us that it is we, the people, who truly are God's Church.

Let's see how you would do if you were given the job of designing a church. What would you put in it? How would it look and whom would it serve? I am going to give you a budget of $500,000. With that money you must build a church building for a congregation of 500 people. The options are listed on the chalkboard. You must have at least two bathrooms. Write down what things your church building will and won't have, what size it will be, etc.

Allow the students five minutes to come up with their model church. Have them share their concepts and ideas with the entire class.

3—Game

 **Materials:** *Club 56 Activity Zone* page 4, dice (three, or spinners with numbers) and prizes (three, small).

We've learned several things today about the early Church. Now you have an opportunity to show what you've learned. Think carefully as you work. There will be prizes for the three students with the most points.

Give the students their *Activity Zone* pages. Have them work individually to answer the questions. When they have answered them, split the class into three groups to play the game. The rules are explained on the worksheet. Have one student on each team keep track of each team member's score.

Bring the class back together and award prizes to the kids with the most points.

4—Outreach Project

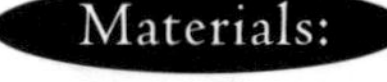 **Materials:** Pencils, papers and envelopes.

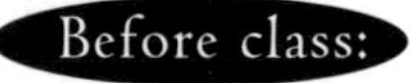 **Before class:** Make a list of pastors of churches in your community. Names of pastors can be found in the yellow pages in the telephone book, church ads in the newspaper or by calling the churches.

Today we learned about the beginning of the Church. We are very blessed by our own church and all the people who work here so that we can come

Activity Zone page 4

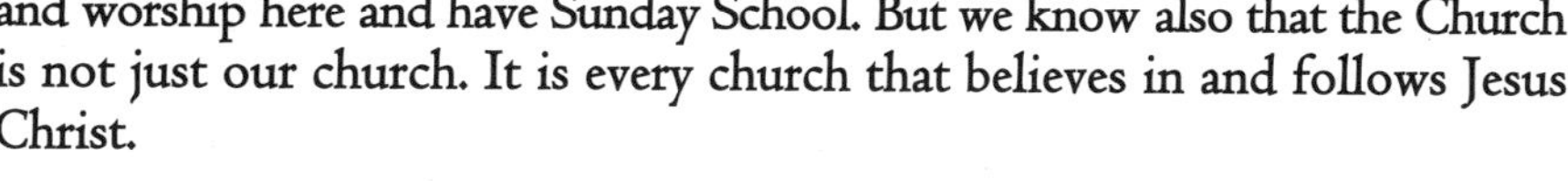

Has God touched you in a super-natural way? Share that experience with your class.

God and people: The real Church.

and worship here and have Sunday School. But we know also that the Church is not just our church. It is every church that believes in and follows Jesus Christ.

Our outreach project today is to write a letter to the pastor of another church in our town and let her know that you appreciate her and are thankful for the job she does to lead people to Christ and to help her church be the Church Alive. Your letter does not need to be lengthy, but should be sincere in its thanks to the pastor. Be sure to tell her why you are writing the letter and that you are from Club 56 at our church.

Give each student the name of a pastor, along with the church name and address.

"Come on, Mom," pleaded Brent. "They even have an air hockey table over at First Church! Please. They do a lot more fun stuff than at our new church." Brent's mother finished typing the last sentence of her letter on the computer. When she looked up at him she seemed troubled.

"Brent, we decided as a family to be part of this brand new church. Each of us understood that we would have to make some sacrifices."

He interrupted her, "I have, Mom. But six months is long enough. I want to go back to First Church. Besides, they don't need me at our little church. I'm the only 6th grader there!"

"Brent, we need to talk to your dad tonight and see what he thinks. In the meantime, I want you to be thinking about the answers to a couple of questions. OK?"

He nodded excitedly. "Sure, Mom," he said, "what are they?" His mother was obviously already on his side. Once she was persuaded, it would be easier to talk his dad into letting him go.

Mom paused for a minute to get his full attention. "First, do you believe that someone your age has a responsibility to the Church? Or, second, because of your age, is the Church more responsible for you? By Church, I mean the body of Christ wherever they might be gathering."

Zap! She'd done it again! This had to be one of those trick questions that kids should always avoid. "Uh, Mom, can you write that down for me?" Brent knew he needed to talk to his friends. He had to come up with good answers before his dad got home from work that night.

Later that afternoon, Brent sat down with his friends Neal and Kyle. "OK, if we can come up with the right answers, I think Mom and Dad will let me go back to First Church. What do you think?"

Neal laughed, "Hey, we're kids. The Church is responsible for us. We still have a lot to learn. When we're older we'll be the ones in charge, and then we'll take responsibility."

Kyle stopped him, "I don't think so. Mom says, 'You learn responsibility by having responsibility.'"

Oh no, thought Brent, *I'm in trouble!* Maybe he did need to stick it out at the new church. But, did they really need a kid? And besides, what about what he wanted? He just wanted to be back with his friends.

What should Brent do?

Brent needed help with his decision. Kyle and Neal each had an opinion. Ask the students to discuss what they believe Kyle and Neal meant.

Then divide the students into small work groups. Assign each group one of the questions in the story to answer. The questions are:

♦ Do you believe that someone your age has a responsibility to the Church?

♦ Is the Church responsible for you because of your age?

There are no right or wrong answers to these questions. Encourage the kids to be thoughtful in their answers. They should think about themselves and their responsibilities, or lack of them, at your church. After the groups have finished, have them report their answers to the whole class.

As a class, decide what Brent should do.

Materials: Copies of *Club 56 Leader's Manual* Lesson 2 ACTS File Page page 25.

Our Power Point today is, *God and people: The real Church.* Your assignment for the Alive Church Technology Services this week is to be an observer and create a report to add to your file that depicts the many people who make up our church. For example, the children in our church are one big group, but they can be broken down into smaller groups such as babies, toddlers, grade school kids, etc. List all the groups you can think of on the borders of your page, then draw a picture of a person on the computer screen. This person will represent our church. Label different parts of the person you drew with the groups of people you've identified. Throughout the week, add to your list as you remember and observe other groups. We will compare the different groups you were able to identify next week.

Be sure to bring your File Pages back with you next week.

Don't be afraid to speak the truth in love to your class. This lesson clearly points out the gospel and the power of the Holy Spirit. Fifth and 6th graders desperately need God's love and power in our society today.

God and people: The real Church.

Alive Church Technology Services

The Church is made up of living, breathing people, not stones and bricks. How many different groups of people can you identify in our church? Think about the different groups who meet together throughout the week. List these groups on the borders of this file page, then draw a picture of a person on the computer screen. This person will represent our church. Label different parts of the person you drew with the groups of people you identified. Throughout the week, add to your list as you remember and observe other groups.

ITEMS NEEDED FOR LESSON

- ❏ ACTS folders
- ❏ Lesson 2 ACTS File Pages

- ❏ Pennies
- ❏ Dimes
- ❏ Bowls (two, identical)
- ❏ Fabric pieces (two, identical)

- ❏ Bibles
- ❏ Bowls with coins (from Opening Activity)
- ❏ Pencils
- ❏ Paper

- ❏ Bibles
- ❏ English muffins
- ❏ Cheddar cheese (grated)
- ❏ Pizza sauce
- ❏ Mozzarella cheese (grated)
- ❏ Pepperoni (sliced)
- ❏ Cookie sheet
- ❏ Rubber spatula
- ❏ Toaster oven (or conventional oven)
- ❏ Index cards
- ❏ Marker

- ❏ None

1—Creative Writing

- ❏ *Club 56 Activity Zone* page 6
- ❏ Pencils

2—Game

- ❏ None

3—Problem Solving

- ❏ *Club 56 Activity Zone* page 5
- ❏ Pencils

4—Individual Art

- ❏ Paper plates
- ❏ Scissors
- ❏ Pencils
- ❏ Yarn
- ❏ Stapler
- ❏ Hole Punch

- ❏ Copies of *Club 56 Leader's Manual* Lesson 3 ACTS File Page page 36

. . . .

SPECIAL NOTE

As you prepare, allow the Holy Spirit to show you how to continue living an incredibly exciting, miraculous, extraordinary life. Be available for miracles this week so that as you teach, your lesson will be alive.

Walking with God: Never a dull moment.

It was the power of Jesus that made this crippled man well. This happened because we trusted in the power of Jesus. You can see this man, and you know him. He was made completely well because of trust in Jesus. You all saw it happen!

Acts 3:16

Acts 3:1-26

A. An Incredibly Exciting Day!

B. An Incredibly Exciting, Miraculous Day!

C. An Incredibly Exciting, Miraculous, Extraordinary Day!

D. Walking With God: Never a Dull Moment

AN INCREDIBLY EXCITING DAY

"Mom," she said hesitantly, "I lost my beautiful birthday necklace at school today." My friend saw the agony on her daughter's lovely face and felt her desperation and sadness.

How could they ever recover a small necklace at a school with 900 students? Anyone could have found and kept it. There was little possibility of ever seeing the special gift again.

In spite of the obvious obstacles, Abby decided she was going to ask God for a miracle. Her mother prayed with her, knowing that this could easily be a very disappointing experience.

For two weeks Abby prayed that God would help her find the necklace she'd received in honor of her tenth birthday. Each day she would remind God of her missing keepsake and thank Him for caring about everything in her life.

One afternoon at her day care, Abby joined the other children on the playground. While she was looking for her friends, she saw Michael working on something small and delicate. Curious, she went to ask what he was doing. He was untangling her heart necklace! Another friend, Katie, had found it, recognized it as Abby's and asked Michael to untangle it before she returned it. Abby was ecstatic! God had worked a miracle for this 10-year-old, and she gave Him thanks. What an incredible day this had turned out to be!

Was it a miracle? Absolutely! Only God could have caused Katie to look down and see the necklace at exactly the right time. Miracles, not coincidences, happen in the lives of believers.

God planted faith in the heart of a 10-year-old girl who knew that she served a powerful and exciting God.

Recognizing miracles is a dynamic and vital part of the Christian walk. Encourage your students to look for the many miracles He performs daily on their behalf, and have an incredibly exciting week!

Materials: ACTS folders and Lesson 2 ACTS File Pages.

Who remembers our Power Point from last week? *God and people: The real Church.* Your assignment for the Alive Church Technology Services was to create a report showing the many groups of people who make up our church. Then you were to draw a picture of a person (representing our church), labeling different parts with the groups of people you identified. Let's see what you came up with.

Have each student show his picture. Note the similarities and differences between each student's body picture.

Have the students put their Lesson 2 ACTS File Pages into their ACTS folders.

Materials: Pennies, dimes, bowls (two, identical) and fabric pieces (two, identical).

Before class: Put dimes in one bowl and pennies in the other. Cover each with fabric. Place the penny bowl on top of the dime bowl so the students do not see both bowls.

Today we are going to participate in an exciting activity. Sometimes projects are boring and dull, but this one is very interesting. Give each student a handful of pennies from the bowl. There is absolutely no talking permitted during this activity after I have given the directions. Your assignment is to take the pennies and line them up by their dates from the oldest to the newest. Allow time to arrange the pennies.

Wasn't that fun? OK, now put them back in the bowl. I don't know when I've had more fun. What did you think of that activity? While the students are discussing the activity, cover the bowl and put it under the dime bowl. This will make it easy to slip out the dime bowl later without students noticing.

No, that activity wasn't really interesting or fun, was it? There was no purpose for the activity or even any conclusion. It was just an average, or even boring, part of your day.

Would you like to have an incredibly exciting day every day? Today in our lesson we're going to see that it's possible. Our Power Point is *Walking with God: Never a dull moment.*

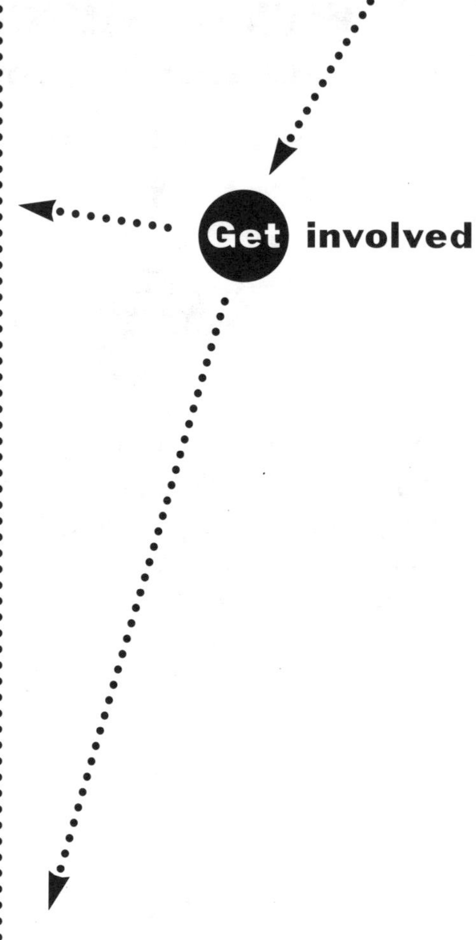

It's OK to be obvious in replacing the bowls as directed. The kids will enjoy the "miracle" on page 30 more that way.

Walking with God: Never a dull moment.

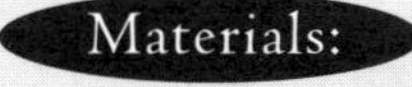

Materials: Bibles, bowls with coins (from Opening Activity), pencils and paper.

An Incredibly Exciting Day

What is the most boring job you've ever done? What made it boring? *(Allow time for discussion.)* Today we're discovering how the New Testament Church continued to be the Church Alive. Today's lesson is from Acts 3:1-10. Find that Scripture in your Bibles and follow along as I read it. *(Read the verses using a strong, dramatic voice.)*

This lame man earned his living by begging. In Bible times there were no social agencies to help sick or poor people. Today we have welfare and convalescent hospitals for people who are ill. In those days, if a person had no family to care for him, every day he would have to find a place to station himself and beg for money. This man had been around for a long time and had found one of the best areas of the city in which to beg. It was right in the path where wealthy people frequently passed.

♦ **What are some ways that beggars get our attention today?** *(Allow students to share experiences they have had.)*

♦ **How did this man get Peter and John to notice him?** *He asked for money.*

♦ **Why do you think they told the man to look at them?** *They wanted his full attention.*

♦ **What do you think he was thinking of as he looked at them?**

Can you imagine his surprise, and probable disappointment, when Peter said he didn't have any money to give him? Then he got an even greater surprise when Peter gave him a gift beyond his wildest imaginations—the ability to walk.

What is the most wonderful surprise you've ever received? Get with a partner quickly and I'll give each person one minute to share your wonderful surprise. *(Warn the students at one minute and then at the end of two minutes. Have two or three students share their story with the whole class.)* Of all the things that could have happened in this man's lifetime, this must have been the most wonderful surprise for him. In an **instant** the lame man's life was changed forever. **Wouldn't you agree that his everyday life suddenly became pretty exciting?** It was an incredibly exciting day for him.

An Incredibly Exciting, Miraculous Day!

Let's read verses 6-8 again. *(Ask a student to do so.)*

♦ **What did Peter need, besides physical strength, to pull the man to his feet?** *Courage and faith in God.*

♦ **How long had this man been unable to walk?** *His whole life.*

◆ **What did the man do when he stood for the first time in his life?** *Stood on his feet, walked, jumped and praised God.*

Have you ever sat on your feet until they went to sleep? How does it feel when you stand up? *(Allow students to answer.)* The lame man had never stood on his feet before. His feet should have felt weird. He should have been unable to balance right away. When he was pulled up, though, he was able to immediately walk and jump in the air! It was a miracle from God! God gave him everything he needed to stand immediately. This was not only an incredibly exciting day, it was an incredibly exciting, miraculous day!

People use the word miracle for a lot of different situations such as, "It was a miracle our team made it to the finals," or "It will be a real miracle if I get a B on this test."

Webster's Dictionary says that a miracle is "an effect or extraordinary event in the physical world which surpasses all known human or natural powers and is ascribed to a supernatural cause." **Would someone explain that in words we can all understand?** *Something that is beyond human or natural ability.*

(Pick up the dime bowl with the fabric over it.) OK, let's take a look at this bowl of pennies. *(Pull off the cover and gasp, showing that the pennies are now dimes.)* **What happened to the pennies? It's a miracle!** *(Allow students to talk while you give each one a dime from the bowl.)* Of course, this isn't a miracle. This wasn't a miracle because the pennies didn't become dimes; I had two bowls, and I simply switched the bowls. An event is not a miracle when there are natural causes.

◆ **How did the townspeople know the lame man's healing wasn't a scam?** *They had known the man since birth.*
◆ **Why do you think God did this miracle?** *He loved the lame man, of course. In addition to that, God was getting the attention of the people. He used this miracle, the first since Jesus' ascension, to let them know that He was alive, powerful and able to work through His people. This miracle was proof from God that any ordinary day could be a day of miracles.*

(Divide the class into small groups and give each group a pencil and piece of paper.) Pretend you are ace reporters for the *Jerusalem Times Gazette.* You have to have an awesome, attention-getting headline for your article on the miracle of the lame man. Your group has two minutes to think of a title that will wow this class. *(Allow the groups to share their titles.)*

An Incredibly Exciting, Miraculous, Extraordinary Day!

Because Peter and John were obedient to God, they were able to talk to a large crowd of people. In verses 11 through 26, Luke tells us that people were so amazed by the miracle that they were interested in anything Peter had to say. Some people even thought the men had performed the healing on their own, but Peter explained that the healing was done by the power of Jesus.

(Have someone read verses 19 and 20.) **What promises did Peter offer the people?** *God would forgive their sins, give them times of spiritual rest and give them Jesus Christ.* Now this day had become an incredibly exciting, miraculous, extraordinary day!

Tell the Bible story with feeling. Share your own experiences as you do so. This helps make the lesson real to the kids.

Walking with God: Never a dull moment.

Walking with God is never dull or boring. God uses ordinary people who are willing to listen and obey. God also uses imperfect people, like you and me. **Do you remember what Peter did to Jesus just prior to Jesus' death?** *Denied Jesus three times.* Even though Peter was too embarrassed to stand with Jesus, God used him with this miracle. No one is beyond God's ability to love and forgive. That is truly another one of God's wonderful miracles. It must have been an incredibly exciting, miraculous, extraordinary day for Peter. God had faith in him.

Walking With God: Never a Dull Moment

Have you ever seen a miracle? *(Encourage the students to share their experiences.)* You might be surprised how many times you've experienced a miracle without even knowing it. Miracles happen continually in the lives of Christians. They might not be enormous like the lame man's being healed, but they are just as powerful and wonderful. *(Share a brief example from your own life.)* **What are some examples of everyday miracles that happen in your lives?** *Healing, protection, finding lost items, etc.*

Our Power Point is *Walking with God: Never a dull moment.* All of the miracles we just talked about can happen in your life every day. Look at the dime that I gave you earlier. Peter looked at the lame man and said, "I don't have any silver or gold, but I do have something else I can give you: By the power of Jesus Christ from Nazareth—stand up and walk!" Take this coin home and put it in a place where it will remind you that you don't need anything but the power of God to experience miracles in your life.

If your spiritual life is dull and needs a little pizzazz, maybe you need to use some Dull Blasters!

Dull Blasters will help you begin to see the miraculous power of God in your life every day. Here are five tested, true, world-famous Dull Blasters:

1. Ask God to make you aware of His presence today.

2. Read your Bible.

3. Listen for His voice.

4. Trust God for courage and faith.

5. Look for opportunities.

Conclusion

Peter and John were on their way to church when God gave them an opportunity to be obedient. They had no way of knowing they were about to have an incredibly exciting day. Because they were willing to do as God directed, they got to be involved in a miracle of healing. If that wasn't enough, they were able to tell an entire crowd of people about Jesus. We, too, can anticipate an exciting adventure with God each day of our lives. Let's ask God to help us.

Father God, thank You for Your love and patience with us. Help us to have the courage to trust You to work miracles through us. Please give us boldness like Peter and John had. Teach us to listen for Your voice and have faith that You will speak to us. We give this coming week to You and ask that You will show us that walking with You is never dull or boring. In Jesus' name, amen.

Materials: Bibles, English muffins, pizza sauce, cheddar cheese (grated), mozzarella cheese (grated), pepperoni (sliced), cookie sheet, rubber spatula, toaster oven (or conventional oven), index cards and marker.

Before class: Write these sentences on five index cards, one per card:

1. It was the power of Jesus that made this crippled man well.
2. This happened because we trusted in the power of Jesus.
3. You can see this man, and you know him.
4. He was made completely well because of trust in Jesus.
5. You all saw it happen!

Today, we talked about the power of trusting in Jesus. Great and miraculous things happen when we listen and respond to God! Now we are going to make a snack that will help us remember today's Memory Verse.

Set up five stations, one with each ingredient at it. Put the rubber spatula with the sauce. Put the cookie sheet at the pepperoni station. Finally, place the index cards at each station as follows: 1-English muffins, 2-pizza sauce, 3-cheddar cheese, 4-mozzarella cheese, 5-pepperoni.

Give students a few minutes to look up and memorize the Memory Verse. When the verse is memorized, they are ready to start the stations. At each station, they must recite the part of the verse that is on the index card. When they are able to do it correctly from memory, they can use the ingredient to make their individual pizzas. Bake the pizzas in the oven at 400° until the cheese is melted, approximately eight minutes. Before the students eat their pizzas, ask the group to repeat the entire verse from memory.

1—Creative Writing

Materials: *Club 56 Activity Zone* page 6 and pencils.

Pass out *Activity Zone* pages and pencils. **God often uses miracles like the story of the lame man's healing to get people's attention. It's a form of advertising! Then God allows His disciples, like you and me, to tell of His love and forgiveness.**

Acts 3:16

It was the power of Jesus that made this crippled man well. This happened because we trusted in the power of Jesus. You can see this man, and you know him. He was made completely well because of trust in Jesus. You all saw it happen!

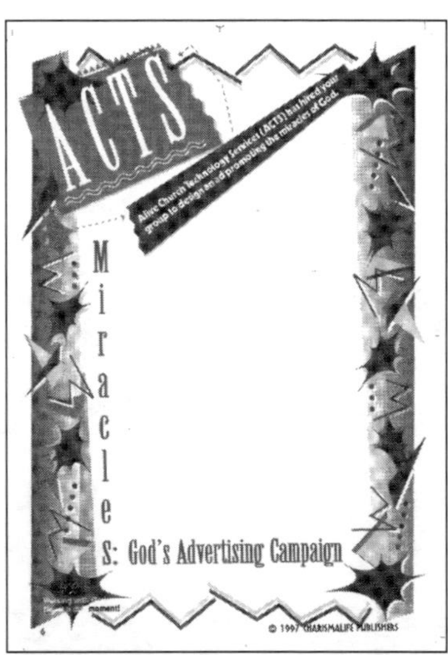

Activity Zone page 6

ACTS (Alive Church Technology Services) has hired you to design and write an ad for its fall catalog that will help sell the miracles of God. Read the Power Point from the *Activity Zone* page before they begin their work. You have five minutes to think of, draw and write your ad.

2—Game

Materials: None.

When Jesus came, He performed many miracles. The good news for us is that miracles didn't stop when He left the earth. His power was imparted through the Holy Spirit so that His disciples could do the same good works. What are some of the miracles Jesus was able to do?

Three specific miracles that Jesus did were to cure a crippled man, to heal the eyes of a blind man and to raise people from the dead! To remind us of these miracles, we are going to play a game.

Clear an area in the room to play the game. Begin by calling out the positions slowly until the students get used to them. Speed up the game as you play to make it silly and fun.

Here is what I want you to do. When I call out "crippled man," I want you to sit on the floor with your legs crossed, just as the crippled man did when he was begging at the city gate. When I call out "blind man," stand up straight and cover your eyes with both of your hands. Finally, when I call out "dead man," fall flat on the ground and play dead. The last person to strike the correct pose will be out of that round.

3—Problem Solving

Materials: *Club 56 Activity Zone* page 5 and pencils.

Have students read the lines about Derek. It's obvious that Derek needs a dose of our world-famous, awesome and incredible Dull Blasters. Unfortunately, Derek doesn't even know they exist. Choose one of the Dull Blasters and write a note to Derek that will explain how it can help him begin to change his life. When you're finished, we will discuss your notes to Derek.

When the students have finished, have them share what they wrote. How many of the Dull Blasters do you presently use in your life? Which will you use this week?

4—Individual Art

Materials: Paper plates, scissors, pencils, yarn, stapler and hole punch.

Our Power Point, *Walking with God: Never a dull moment,* is easy to understand, but we are not always in the middle of the kind of excitement witnessed by the early Church. We do need to be ready to respond to God when He works through us. Today we will make something to help us remember that God wants to have a hand in our lives—He wants to direct us and give us specific directions for each day.

Pass out two paper plates, scissors and a pencil to each student. Students should trace their hand onto the center of one plate and carefully cut out the handprint.

Walking with God: Never a dull moment.

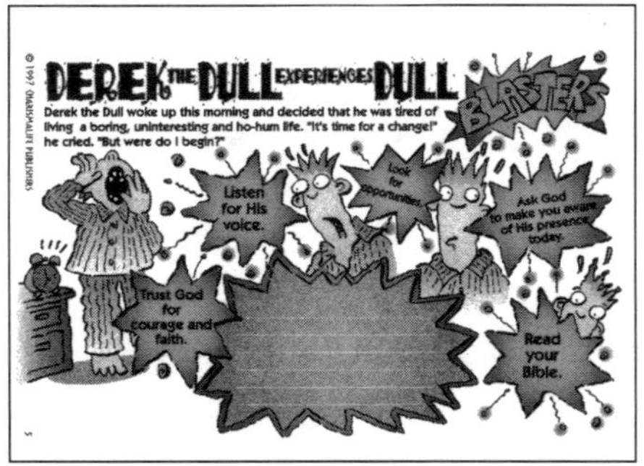

Activity Zone page 5

Have them write words to remind them of the five Dull Blasters on the cutout hand. (Dull Blasters are listed in "Walking With God: Never a Dull Moment" of the Bible Lesson, as well as on *Activity Zone* page 5.)

They should tape the paper plate back together where they cut in from the side. Have them staple the cutout plate to another paper plate so they are top-to-top, not stacked. Have them write "God wants a hand in my life." on the plate with the hand-shaped cutout.

Have students punch a hole in the top of the hand cutout and the top and bottom of the stapled plates. Have students tie a 6-inch piece of yarn to the top hole on the plates and a 4-inch piece between the plates and the hand. The hand should hang below the plates.

Let this mobile be a reminder to you of God's hand in your life. Sometimes you can see His work and sometimes you can't. Yet He is always there. Use the Dull Blasters to help you see Him at work in your life. Hang this mobile at home in a place where you will see it often.

Melody sighed bleakly, "I have the most boring life in the world. Nothing exciting ever happens to me!"

Lisa laughed, "That's not true! Just last week you got another frog for your aquarium." They laughed, but Melody's delight quickly turned into a frown. She flung open the curtain in her bedroom and looked out. "I want to have something absolutely spectacular happen to me."

"So," asked Lisa, "what do you have in mind?"

Melody was thoughtful for a moment. "Oh, something like winning a trip to Europe or saving someone from drowning."

"Well," said Lisa, "right now we have to get to soccer practice. Let's go."

They were the last ones to arrive at the practice that evening. "Hi, girls," said Mr. Frank. "Is everyone ready to show me her incredible progress?"

The girls lined up to kick balls down the field. They were halfway down the field when they heard a cry. It was accompanied by the chilling sound of a bone snapping. Melody looked over to see her friend Lisa lying on the ground, writhing in pain. Melody ran over immediately and knelt down. The other girls gathered around. "Lisa, Lisa," cried Melody, "are you all right?"

Mr. Frank pushed back the girls and knelt in front of them. "Lisa, where does it hurt?" She cried and pointed to her ankle. Mr. Frank took one look and realized he needed to get her to the hospital. "I'm going to the phone," he explained. "I need someone to go to my car and get a blanket to put over Lisa. Melody, just try to comfort her and keep her down." He ran toward the parking lot.

As students work, talk with each one quietly. Ask about his past week, school, family, etc.

Walking with God: Never a dull moment.

"Melody, help me!" sobbed Lisa. She grabbed Melody's arm and held it tight. "My leg hurts so bad! I can't move it. Make it stop hurting, please. You know how to pray. Please ask Jesus to help me!"

Melody was stunned. This wasn't what she meant when she said she wanted something exciting to happen. She didn't pray out loud in public. *What should I say?* she wondered. Everyone was watching her expectantly. She tried to think of the right words, but her mind was blank. Why hadn't she listened better when others prayed? *Are there special words?* she wondered. She prayed silently for help from God.

What do you think happened?

Melody believed that God would heal Lisa. Her concern was knowing how to pray in an emergency.

Divide the students into small groups to discuss the following questions:

♦ What might happen if Melody prayed and Lisa's pain got worse?

♦ What might be hard about praying in front of the other girls?

♦ How can being able to pray make your life more exciting?

♦ Should you pray out loud for someone if they haven't asked?

After the discussion, have them role-play praying for a friend who is in pain.

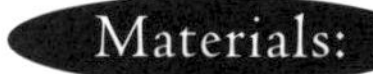
Materials: Copies of *Club 56 Leader's Manual* Lesson 3 ACTS File Page page 36.

Miracles come in all shapes and sizes. Your Challenge this week is to create computer screen icons that could be used for people to access files about miracles. Interview at least five people in your church about miracles they have experienced firsthand. Write brief descriptions of the experiences on the back of your page. Create a symbol for each of the miracles described and draw it on the computer screen.

For example, if someone shares about God giving them money in a miraculous way, you could draw the symbol for money. Next week we'll check out the different icons everyone came up with.

Be sure to bring your File Pages back with you next week. We will add them to your ACTS folders.

Encourage students to take the Challenge and return their File Pages by offering a small reward for all returned File Pages next week.

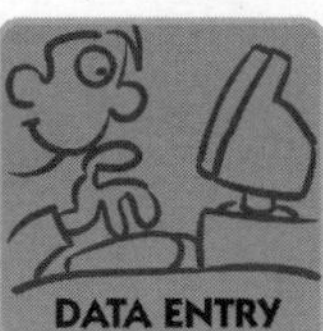

Alive Church Technology Services

Interview at least five people in your church about miracles they have experienced firsthand. Write brief descriptions of the experiences on the back of this File Page. Create a symbol for each of the miracles described and draw it on the computer screen. For example, if someone shares about God giving them money in a miraculous way, you could draw the symbol for money.

Lesson 3 ACTS File Page

Dear Club 56 Leaders,

Welcome to the Club 56 Acts quarter of lessons. I trust that you will find, as I have, that God has anointed our writers and designers to bring together an excellent teaching tool for you, the Church's 5th and 6th grade leaders.

Here are some helps and suggestions before you begin teaching:

◊ Throughout these lessons, a difference in capitalization is made between "the Church," referring to all believers regardless of denomination and "the church," referring to any local congregation, including yours.

◊ Your class will take home an assignment from the Alive Church Technology Services (ACTS) each week. They will be researching how your church can continue to be a part of the Church Alive. In Lesson 13, your pastor is invited to come in and hear the students' conclusions. We strongly recommend you use this tool to enhance the relationship your pastor and students have with each other, as well as help them encourage and prompt each other to continue walking in a real, live way with God.

◊ Two sample tracts were included with this manual: one a kids' guide to witnessing and the other a kids' guide to spiritual encounters. These are excellent references to use with 5th and 6th graders, as well as younger-aged children. Both of these tracts are referenced in the lessons (11 and 8 respectively).

◊ As you prepare and teach these 13 lessons, be aware of the Holy Spirit's guidance to be the Church Alive among your family, friends, students in Club 56 and other members of your church. Let the truth of the lessons touch your innermost being before you teach them. You will teach more effectively as you communicate what you have already experienced in your own life.

Have a great quarter being the Church Alive with your 5th and 6th graders!

In Him,

Laurie Dickerson

Laurie Dickerson
Club 56 Editor

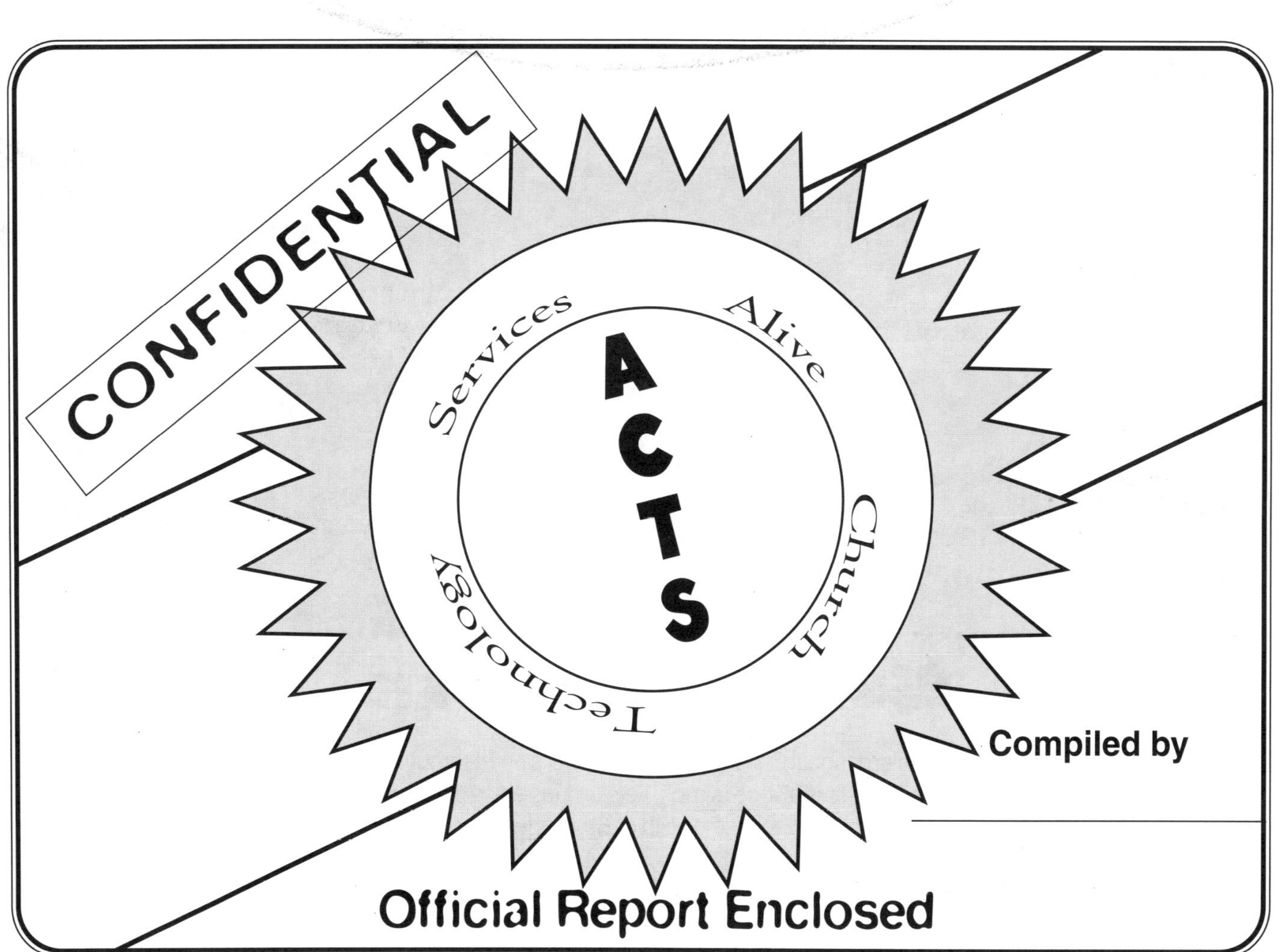

ITEMS NEEDED FOR LESSON

- ❑ ACTS folders
- ❑ Lesson 3 ACTS File Pages

1—Problem Solving

- ❑ None

2—Bible Study

- ❑ *Club 56 Activity Zone* page 7
- ❑ Bibles
- ❑ Pencils

- ❑ Index cards
- ❑ Pencils

3—Object Lesson

- ❑ Jars (small, with lids)
- ❑ Pitcher
- ❑ Measuring cup
- ❑ Measuring spoons
- ❑ Glitter (metallic)
- ❑ Sand
- ❑ Water
- ❑ Oil

- ❑ Bibles
- ❑ Paper (lightweight)

4—Group Art

- ❑ *Club 56 Activity Zone* page 9
- ❑ Bibles
- ❑ Markers
- ❑ Construction paper
- ❑ Hole punch
- ❑ Paper fasteners

- ❑ Bibles
- ❑ Ball
- ❑ Chalk
- ❑ Chalkboard

- ❑ None

- ❑ Copies of *Club 56 Leader's Manual* Lesson 4 ACTS File Page page 49

SPECIAL NOTE

The International Children's Version Bible is used throughout *Club 56.* This is a good, simple version kids enjoy. Encourage parents to buy these for their 5th or 6th graders for Christmas, birthdays, etc.

Know what you believe and believe what you know.

Jesus is the only One who can save people. His name is the only power in the world that has been given to save people. And we must be saved through him!

Acts 4:12

Acts 4:3-22; Mark 2:10-12; Luke 24:27; John 6:51; 10:25-33; 14:6-7; 21:24; 1 Corinthians 15:12-20; 2 Timothy 3:16; 1 Peter 1:25; 2 Peter 1:21

A. Certainly Not Dull!

B. So You're a Christian?

C. The Bible: Believable?

D. Jesus: the Real Thing?

E. Resurrection: Reality or Hoax?

DEFEND YOUR FAITH!

"You're one of those Christians, aren't you, Nancy?" I looked up to see my high school social studies teacher standing over me in the library. I glanced around the table at my friends, wondering what was up.

"Yes," I slowly replied. With that short answer, I was given the assignment of presenting the Christian faith to the comparative religions class I was taking. The teacher in question thought I would do a better job of it than he would since he didn't believe in Christ.

With great naiveté, but also the great confidence only found in the young, I plunged into my preparations. During that time, I had many occasions to be thankful for the strong foundation I had received from my years in Sunday School. Bible stories and Memory Verses were still hiding in the recesses of my brain. The many lessons that had been taught to me were dusted off and given new life. My teachers had done well in preparing me to share what I believed. For a week I presented the Christian faith to my classmates in the public school system.

Club 56 is a perfect opportunity to stretch and grow your students in their faith. Check their foundation to make sure it is strong. Shore up any cracks that might have appeared. Continue to build on what they know. Help them as they grow in what they believe.

Materials: ACTS folders and Lesson 3 ACTS File Pages.

What was our Power Point last week? *Walking with God: Never a dull moment.* Your Challenge this week was to interview people who had experienced miracles and then create computer screen icons representing those miracles.

What were the miracles you heard about? Have students share the stories they wrote and the icons they drew to represent them.

♦ Did any of you experience miracles this week?
♦ Did you use any or all of the world-famous Dull Blasters?
♦ How was your walk with God exciting this week?

Have students put their Lesson 3 ACTS File Pages into their ACTS folders.

Materials: Index cards and pencils.

There are many things we believe in, even though we may not understand them. For example, I believe in electricity. Although I can't see it or even tell you much about how it works, I know it is real because I can see how it works. If I walk over to a light switch and turn it on, I have faith that the light will come on. I can't actually see the electricity flowing through the wires; I don't know how it comes to my house through the lines or how it was harnessed from water or by nuclear means, but my act of flipping the light switch shows that I have faith, or belief, that it will come on.

What are some other things like electricity that we believe in without knowing a lot about how they work? Think for a moment about some things you believe in. Think about both everyday things and things you believe about God. As you think of them, write them on your index card.

Give the students a moment to come up with ideas. When they are finished, have the students share what they wrote down.

♦ What does it take for you to believe in the things you wrote down? *Usually faith in the process.* Have students answer about each item on their list.
♦ How does faith help you in believing?

Our lesson today is about what we believe about God, Jesus and the Holy Spirit. As the early church was beginning, there were many times when it was called upon to defend its message. We, too, must be able to give an answer for what we believe.

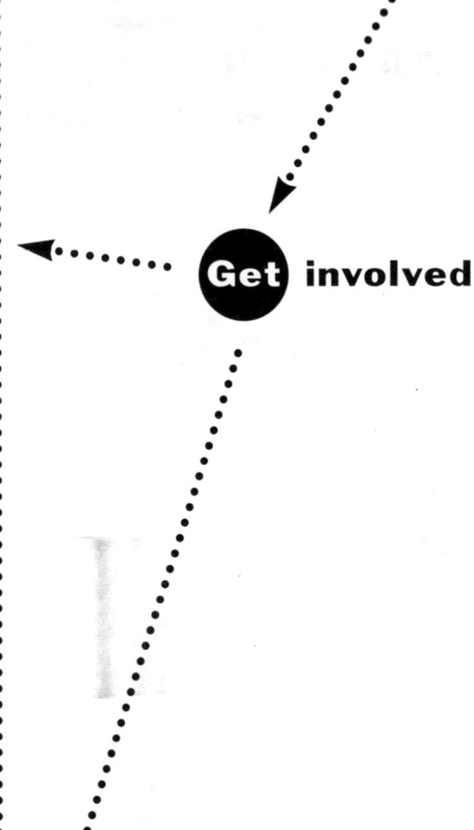

Know what you believe and believe what you know.

Directions for folding Origami Fish

Step 1

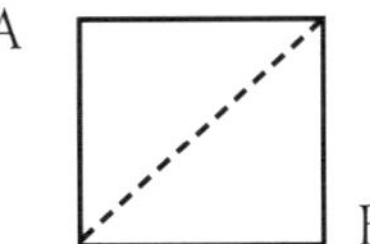

Begin with a square piece of lightweight paper. Bring A to B, folding the square diagonally. Crease. Open the paper.

Step 2

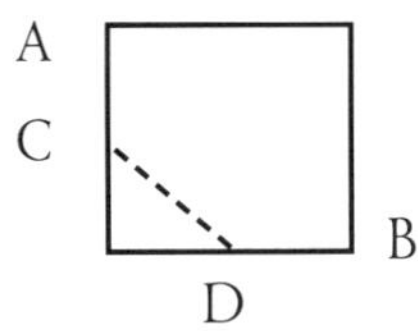

Fold line C-D to the center.

Step 3

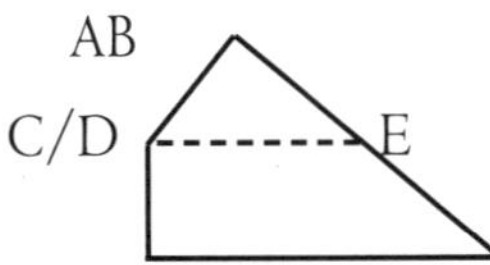

Keeping that fold, refold A to B.

Fold point A and point B outside along line C/D - E.

Step 4

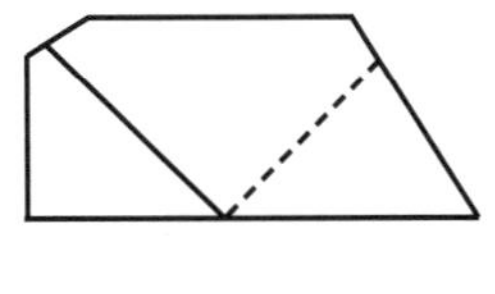

Fold points C and D to the inside as shown.

Fold point G up along the dotted line.

Step 5

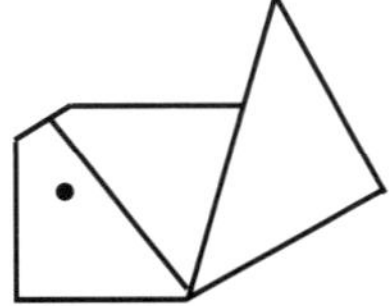

Draw an eye on the completed fish.

Materials: Bibles and paper (lightweight).

Before class: Fold an origami fish and hide it in your pocket. Instructions and illustrations for folding are in the column.

Certainly Not Dull!

Just as we learned last week, Peter and John were not having dull days. Since the man was healed, they were actually getting into trouble with the Jewish leaders. Let's find out what happened.

(Have volunteers read Acts 4:3,5-12,16-22.) The Jewish leaders put Peter and John in jail, then took them in for questioning.

What did you like best about how Peter responded to the leaders in verses 8-12? *(Allow students to answer.)* One of the things we can see from this section of Scripture is that Peter knew what he believed, and he wasn't afraid to share it, even though the consequence could have been great. As it turned out, the only consequence was spending one night in jail. The Jewish leaders couldn't put them in jail permanently.

♦ **What did they tell Peter and John not to do?** *Speak or teach in the name of Jesus.*

♦ **How did Peter and John respond?**

It's important for all of us to know what we believe and believe what we know. Let's take a close look at some things we believe about God.

So You're a Christian?

What does it mean to be a Christian? *(Allow a few minutes to discuss this.)*

The term "Christian" was first applied to people in Antioch who believed that Jesus Christ had died for their sins. They were called this because they were followers of Christ and His teachings. The word "Christian" actually means "little Christ." This term helped distinguish the Christians from the other religious people of the day who believed in God but did not accept what Jesus had said.

Do you ever question or struggle with your own faith? Do you ever wonder if you might be wrong? Could you explain your faith if someone questioned you? *(Allow students to answer.)* Let's look into some tough questions about our faith. We'll research them and see if we can come up with answers for them.

♦ Is the Bible true and reliable?

♦ Is Jesus who He said He was?

♦ Did Jesus really die and rise again?

The Bible: Believable?

Our first question is about the book that gives us most of our information about the things we believe: the Bible. If we trust the Bible, then we can believe the information it gives us. However, many people can't accept that the Bible is really the Word of God or that the information it contains is true.

Here are some facts about the Bible. It was written over a period of about 1,500 years by more than 40 different authors. Some of the authors of the Bible we know, but many we don't. The authors that we know about came from a variety of backgrounds. There were generals, fishermen, prophets, kings and a doctor, to name just a few.

Even though the Bible contains many different books and was written by different people over a long period of time, the theme never changed. The Bible reveals to us God's plan of salvation in the Old Testament and the fulfillment of the plan in the New Testament.

Let's find out some things the Bible has to say about the Bible.

(Have the students look up the following verses to read out loud.) As we read and listen to these verses, think about how they can help convince you that the Bible is believable.

- ◊ Luke 24:27
- ◊ 1 Peter 1:25
- ◊ John 21:24
- ◊ 2 Peter 1:21
- ◊ 2 Timothy 3:16

There are other arguments to support the Bible, too. As you listen to them, think about which you might share with a friend who is wondering if the Bible is true. Here are four:

1. Jesus quoted from the Scripture and used it to verify who He was. There are over 40 prophecies about Him that were made in the Old Testament hundreds of years before He was born. Jesus was the only person to fulfill them all.

2. Support comes from early manuscripts. There are manuscripts of Scripture, such as the Dead Sea Scrolls, that date back to the first century. These are in museums now. The manuscripts were translated and put in the form of books, chapters and verses in our Bibles. All of the information in these manuscripts agrees with and authenticates our Bibles. There has never been any old manuscript found that does not agree with the words which our Bible contains. There are more than 5,000 Greek manuscripts from which our present-day Bible was derived.

3. There are many prophecies, such as in the book of Daniel, that predicted events hundreds of years before they happened. These all came true and were accurately fulfilled.

4. There is also archaeological evidence. No evidence has ever been uncovered to disprove the Bible. Instead, the reverse has happened. As explorations of the Holy Land continue, scientists find more evidence that supports the Bible as we have it now.

Watch and pray for students who can't or don't concentrate on the lesson or activity at hand. Ask the Lord to show you how to get them involved.

Know what you believe and believe what you know.

Discussions are boring if they are one-sided. Make sure that your students are being pulled into the talk by allowing them freedom to voice their opinions, whatever those opinions are.

Jesus: the Real Thing?

Believing in the Bible is central to our faith. So much of what it has to say to us points to the person of Jesus. **But how do we know that Jesus is the Son of God?** *(After you have allowed the class to respond a little, interrupt the discussion by saying you need a moment to check on the fish in your pocket.)*

What, you don't believe I have a fish in my pocket? Why not? *(Allow the students to respond. They will probably say things like: fish could not survive in a pocket, no one would walk around with a fish in her pocket, etc.)* **I'm hurt that you don't believe me. Have I ever lied to you before? What does it take to trust somebody?** *A past history with the person that shows she is trustworthy and honest.* **How many of you believe me, not thinking about my outrageous claim, but simply basing your belief on what you know about me?** Well, those of you who chose to believe me are right. I do have a fish in my pocket. *(Show the origami fish.)* OK, it's not a live one, but I never said it was. Let me show you how to fold one of these. *(Following the directions given earlier in the lesson, have each student fold a fish.)*

Hopefully this demonstration illustrated something important to you. Part of believing someone is being able to trust her. Even though Jesus made some amazing claims, He always fulfilled them. Jesus lived His life in such a way that He proved He is trustworthy. Let's look at three other reasons that help to support Jesus' claim to be God's Son.

1. The Bible supports Jesus. We have already made a defense to prove the accuracy of the Bible. Therefore, we can accept what the Bible records about Jesus being the Son of God.

2. The four Gospels record the same story—of Jesus' birth, life, death and resurrection—even though they were written by four different authors at different times and places. Again, since we have proven that the Bible is true, we can trust the Gospels, which are part of that Bible.

3. The disciples believed Jesus. These men were Jesus' closest friends. They worked with Him and watched what He did. Someone might say, "They were liars. Maybe they thought that by going along with Jesus they would become rich and famous." If we follow that line of thinking, then all we have to do is look at the lives of the disciples. **Did they become wealthy or powerful? Did they have the kind of lives that others were envious of?** The answer to both questions is "No!". The disciples gave up everything to follow Jesus. Most of them, in the end, forfeited their lives. **Would someone be willing to die for a lie?** *It's not likely.*

So, since we have proven that Jesus was really who He said He was—the Son of God—then we can also trust the claims that He made. Let's look into some of the statements Jesus made about Himself. *(Have the students look up the following verses.)*

◊ John 10:25
◊ John 10:31-33
◊ Mark 2:10-12
◊ John 6:51
◊ John 14:6-7

Wow, those are some pretty awesome claims.

♦ Do you think they are all true?

♦ Can you accept the things that Jesus said about Himself?

Resurrection: Reality or Hoax?

At the very center of the Christian faith is the idea that Jesus died to save us, then rose from the dead. Many people say they can believe that Jesus died, but it's the coming back to life that they struggle with. Some might say, "What does it matter? Just accept that Jesus was a good person and a great teacher." If you buy that, listen while I read these verses to you. *(Read 1 Cor. 15:12-14,20.)*

There is no middle ground here. Jesus either did what He said He had come to do—died for all of us and rose from the dead—or He was a fraud. If He didn't fulfill all the claims He spoke, He is not a great teacher, but a liar. Great teachers are not people who lie to people.

The disciples and the early Church knew Jesus to be who He said He was. They believed Him so fully that they were willing to be put to death for the message they spoke. *(Read Acts 4:12.)* This was the message that the disciples gave to all who would listen. It wasn't just words; it was what they knew to be true.

Conclusion

It's not wrong to have questions about your faith. Questioning is one way you will come to understand what you believe. When you seek answers, it helps you grow. It will also help you when you have to defend why you believe in God, the Bible and Jesus Christ. We all need to know what we believe and believe what we know. As a matter of fact, that's our Power Point today: ***Know what you believe and believe what you know.*** **Why don't you say that with me?** *(Have students repeat it several times until they know it well. Pray with the class, asking God to help them grow in their faith and in understanding some of the facts that their faith is based on.)*

Materials: Bibles, ball, chalk and chalkboard.

Our Memory Verse today can be found in Acts 4:12. Have several students read the verse from their Bibles. As they are reading, write it on the board. Have the students form a circle. Give one student the ball.

Now we will recite the Memory Verse as the ball is passed around. First, let's pass the ball around the circle slowly a few times. Each time you receive the ball you must say the next word in the Memory Verse. I have written it up here on the chalkboard.

Relationship with God through Jesus Christ is based on faith, not facts. Help students realize that knowing the facts is the basis for defending their faith, not for having faith.

Acts 4:12

Jesus is the only One who can save people. His name is the only power in the world that has been given to save people. And we must be saved through him!

As you get better, I will instruct you to begin speeding up. You will also be allowed to pass the ball to anyone in the circle. Also, I am going to start erasing one word at a time of the verse.

Play until the verse is completely erased from the board and the class can say it.

Know what you believe and believe what you know.

1—Problem Solving

Materials: None.

In our Bible Lesson and Memory Verse, it is made very clear that there is only one way to be saved—through believing in Jesus. Sometimes people have a hard time believing this. They think it sounds too easy. Today people try many other ways to get to heaven.

♦ What are some things people believe in and try to do to find salvation? *Being good, improving themselves, meditation, crystals, etc.*

What is our Power Point today? *Know what you believe and believe what you know.* I'm going to give you an opportunity to practice this Power Point. You and your group will have three minutes to decide how to defend what you believe to a certain kind of person. Try to think of Scripture to help support your belief. You can ask me if you're stumped for a Scripture, and I will try to help you. Scripture references follow each of the descriptions. Give these only if the kids can't think of any.

Divide the students into four groups. Assign each group one of the people below. Give the groups three minutes to problem-solve, then discuss each group's solution as a class.

♦ How would you defend the gospel…

◊ to a friend who believed she could go to heaven by being good? *Acts 4:12*

◊ to a friend who believes that everyone will go to heaven? *Matthew 7:21-23*

◊ to a friend who says there is no heaven or hell? *Matthew 25:34,41*

◊ to a friend who says it doesn't matter whether you believe in Jesus Christ and God, as long as you believe in something? *Acts 4:12*

2—Bible Study

Materials: *Club 56 Activity Zone* page 7, Bibles and pencils.

It is important to know what we believe. It is also important to know why we believe as we do—that our beliefs are not just something we invented or made up. We need to know the foundation for our beliefs.

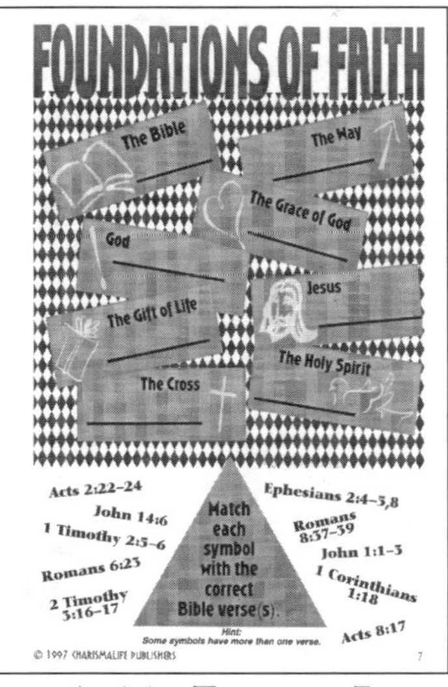

Activity Zone page 7

Hand out the *Activity Zone* page. The students will use their Bibles to explore the foundation of some basic Christian beliefs.

3—Object Lesson

 **Materials:** Jars (small, with lids), pitcher, measuring cup, measuring spoons, glitter (metallic), sand, water and oil.

Have the students work in small groups of two or three. Give each group a jar. Here is what they are to do:

1. Put 2 teaspoons of the glitter into a jar.

2. Add 2 tablespoons of sand.

3. Shake to mix together.

You now have assembled an object lesson. Here is the problem I want you to solve: How would you now separate the worthless sand from the more valuable glitter? You have one minute to try to come up with a solution. Allow students to work with their groups.

Did you come up with an answer? Allow the groups to share their solutions. Was it difficult to try to figure out what might work?

Would it help if I gave you a little help? Try this.

1. Add 1 cup of water.
2. Add 2 tablespoons of oil.
3. Shake the jar vigorously.
4. Let everything settle.

Solution: The glitter will cling to the oil particles. The oil, which does not dissolve in water, floats to the surface. The glitter floats to the surface with the oil.

This object lesson is a good demonstration of our lesson for today. We are going to hear a lot of ideas in our lives. We need to be able to pull out the ones that are true and valuable. The others we need to let sink to the bottom of our lives.

4—Group Art

Materials: *Club 56 Activity Zone* page 9, Bibles, markers, construction paper, hole punch and paper fasteners.

It is important to know what we believe. It is also important that we are able to communicate what we believe to others. Most churches have some sort of statement of faith that will list the things they believe.

♦ What are some of the things we believe here in Club 56?
♦ How would somebody coming into our classroom find out what we believe?

Let's work together as a group to come up with a book that would list the things we believe. I will assign your group one section of our book. Each person in your group will contribute one page to that section. When we're done we will put the book together and display it in the room so that any new person coming in here could look at it and know what we believe.

Experiments are fun for 5th and 6th graders. Make sure they make the connection between what they are doing and the point of the lesson.

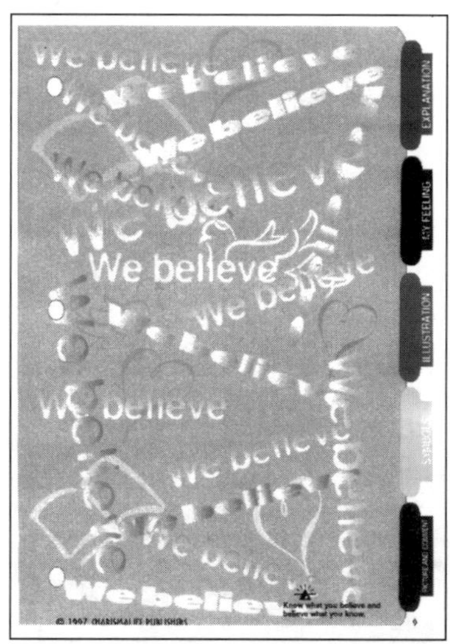

Activity Zone page 9

Give students their *Activity Zone* pages. Review the points from the lesson about things that we, as Christians, believe. Assign each group a belief to illustrate. Each group can talk about and decide how they want to communicate their point. Each person in the group should express the point in some way on her worksheet. She can write it out, support it with Scripture or come up with an artistic interpretation. Have her cut off the extra tabs, leaving the one that identifies her page correctly. The group also needs to design a construction paper title page to their section.

When the students have completed their pages, align all the pages, with each group's page behind their title page and all groups' pages together. Punch holes on the left side. Fasten the pages together with the paper fasteners to form a book. Find a place to display the book in your classroom.

Know what you believe and believe what you know.

Hi, I'm Brock Allen Richardson. Eventually there will be an M.D. after that name, but I don't have time to tell you about my future career right now.

I have just had the most embarrassing moment in my life. No, I didn't make a strange sound that was mistaken for a bodily function.

Here's what happened: My mom asked if I wanted to go with her to the store. Of course I didn't! She left after she gave me the five-minute speech on how to handle all emergencies.

A few minutes later I heard the doorbell ring. I went to the door, and there were these two really big guys. They asked if my mom was home, and I told them that she would be right back.

They looked pretty harmless. You know the kind—clean-cut and well dressed. I wondered out loud if my mom was expecting them, but they said no. So I started to get really curious. I asked them what they wanted at our house.

They were really nice, so I had already figured out they must be Christians. And sure enough, they said they were on a mission for God for a whole year before they started college. Let me tell you, these guys looked like a couple of football players! I thought it was really neat that they chose to put God first before going to college.

I asked them if they would like a cold drink. They said they couldn't come inside my house because my mom wasn't home, but that a big glass of water would be great.

After I got their water we sat on the front lawn and talked. They knew a lot about God. They even said that one day we would all become gods. I wonder why they never told me that at church? Before they left, they offered to come back and talk to my mom about having me take a class with them.

Well, when my mom got home, I told her about our really cool guests. I told her all about us becoming gods. I thought she'd be wowed like I was, but she didn't look impressed at all. She looked concerned. Then she started talking.

She couldn't believe that I didn't know there is only one God, and I'm not Him and am never going to be Him. She explained to me how their beliefs were different from ours—and I mean, really different! They didn't even believe that Jesus Christ is the only Son of God.

So, how was I supposed to know that those guys didn't really believe like us? It was kind of scary 'cause I sort of believed everything they said. How could I tell the difference? All of a sudden I could see why I ought to know the Bible and what I believe.

What would you do if that happened to you?

Discuss the following questions in your large group.

♦ What are some questions that Brock might have asked the men about their faith to help clarify their position?

♦ Not all Christians believe the same things. What are some of the important issues Christians must believe to truly be Christians?

♦ Why might it help you to know what other religions believe?

Divide the class into small work groups. Have the students role-play dealing with door-to-door religionists or answering questions about their faith. When the roleplays are complete, give the students an opportunity to tell about times they have been able to share their faith with others.

Know what you believe and believe what you know.

Materials: Copies of *Club 56 Leader's Manual* Lesson 4 ACTS File Page page 49.

What is our Power Point today? *Know what you believe and believe what you know.* People believe many different things about God and Jesus. Your Challenge from the Alive Church Technology Services this week is to poll ten kids your age, some who are Christians and some who are not. Find out three things each of them believe about Jesus. Make notes of what they say.

Take their comments and design a poster for churches to display in their classrooms to help 5th and 6th graders understand what others believe. Draw your design on the screen on your page. We will share our posters with each other next week.

Be sure to bring these File Pages back with you next week.

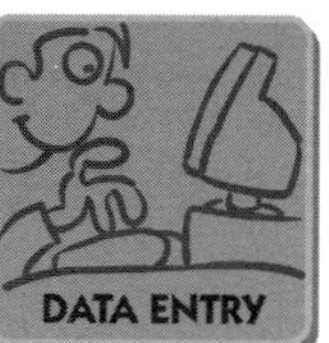

Alive Church Technology Services

This week, ask ten people your age to tell you three things (each) they believe about Jesus. You will need to ask five people who you know are Christians and five people who you are pretty sure are not. Design a poster on the screen. On your poster, list things Christians your age believe, as well as things kids your age who aren't Christians believe.

ITEMS NEEDED FOR LESSON

challenge review

❑ ACTS folders
❑ Lesson 4 ACTS File Pages

opening activity

❑ Watch (with a second hand)

bible lesson

❑ Bibles
❑ Index cards
❑ Marker
❑ Fitness video
❑ Picture of the White House
❑ Director's chair (or folding chair labeled "Director")

memory verse activity

❑ Bibles
❑ String (or yarn)
❑ Cups (large, Styrofoam)
❑ Scissors

living it out

❑ None

more activities

1—Bible Study

❑ *Club 56 Activity Zone* page 8
❑ Bibles
❑ Pencils

2—Cooking

❑ 7-Up (in 1- or 2-liter containers)
❑ Sherbet (any flavor)
❑ Cups
❑ Ice cream scoop
❑ Napkins

3—Individual Art

❑ Paper (thin, white)
❑ Crayons
❑ Cookie sheets (four, with sides)
❑ Jello (four 3-ounce boxes, different colors)
❑ Hot water   ❑ Measuring cups
❑ Spoon   ❑ Vegetable oil
❑ Newspaper   ❑ Hair dryer

4—Outreach

❑ *Club 56 Activity Zone* page 11
❑ Bibles
❑ Envelopes
❑ Stamps
❑ List of church leaders

challenge for the week

❑ Copies of *Club 56 Leader's Manual* Lesson 5 ACTS File Page page 61

SPECIAL NOTE

Pictures, such as the one called for in the Bible Lesson, can be obtained from encyclopedias, newspapers, magazines or the Internet.

Leadership: Part of God's plan for powerful ministry.

So, brothers, choose seven of your own men. They must be men who are good. They must be full of wisdom and full of the Spirit. We will put them in charge of this work. Then we can use all our time to pray and to teach the word of God.

Acts 6:3-4

Acts 6:1-7

A. Leaders of the Pack
B. Leading the "God" Way
C. A Child Shall Lead Them—You!

ARE THERE ANY LEADERS IN THE HOUSE?

He hung up the telephone, then called my name. I knew I was in for a serious lecture and severe punishment. I braced myself for the worst, knowing Dad had just found out I had snuck out of my cabin after curfew at a youth retreat the previous weekend.

Instead, my father calmly said, "I am really disappointed in you." He paused for what seemed like hours, then said, "I want you to write a paper for me about your decision to sneak out and how it dishonored the leadership God placed over you. I recommend you use your Bible as a reference."

A writing assignment? This was worse than being forbidden from using the phone or going out with friends. My father knew of my dream of becoming a writer and of the hours I spent journaling every thought in my 15-year-old brain. Making the very thing I loved into a punishment was brilliant.

As I wrote, conviction grew in my heart. I recognized that I had blatantly disobeyed God's Word and the people He had placed in my life to love and guide me. Through the assignment, I also recognized that my father was an excellent leader. He had assisted me in developing a righteous perspective about my actions, led me to God's Word to better understand why what I had done was wrong and directed me to use my gift and love for writing for something that would make a difference in my response to leadership forever.

You are part of God's plan for ministry. You are the leader chosen to share this lesson with the 5th and 6th graders in your class. Ask the Lord to help you use the creative ways in this lesson to effectively communicate His purpose for leadership within the Church. Ask Him to sharpen your leadership skills and discernment so you can encourage and motivate the young leaders in your class.

challenge review

Materials: ACTS folders and Lesson 4 ACTS File Pages.

This week the Alive Church Technology Services asked you to be a designer. What was our Power Point last week? *Know what you believe and believe what you know.* You were to design a poster that would help 5th and 6th graders know what people believe, both Christians and non-Christians.

♦ Whom did you poll?

♦ What was the most interesting thing a Christian 5th or 6th grader believed in?

♦ What was the most interesting thing a non-Christian 5th or 6th grader believed in?

♦ What kind of poster did you make to go in your ACTS file?

Have each student show his poster, then put it in his ACTS folder.

opening activity

Materials: Watch (with a second hand).

We're going to play a game called "Line Leader." For the next three minutes, each of you is going to try to be the line leader for our class. The person who is at the front of the line when the three minutes is over will be the winner.

To get to the front of the line, think of a type of leader in our country. Your answer could be a leader from a church, the government, a school, the community, etc. Examples of acceptable answers are: teachers, police chiefs, pastors, etc. You cannot repeat someone else's answer.

Have students remain seated until they offer an answer. The first student to raise his hand and give an answer starts the line. The next person to answer takes the front of the line and so on. All students can give answers, even if they are already in line. At the end of three minutes, declare the person at the front of the line the winner.

Was it fun to be the leader? Allow students to talk about the game. **Today we will be focusing on leadership in the Church.** We will look at God's plan for leadership from the book of Acts and ways you can develop your leadership skills.

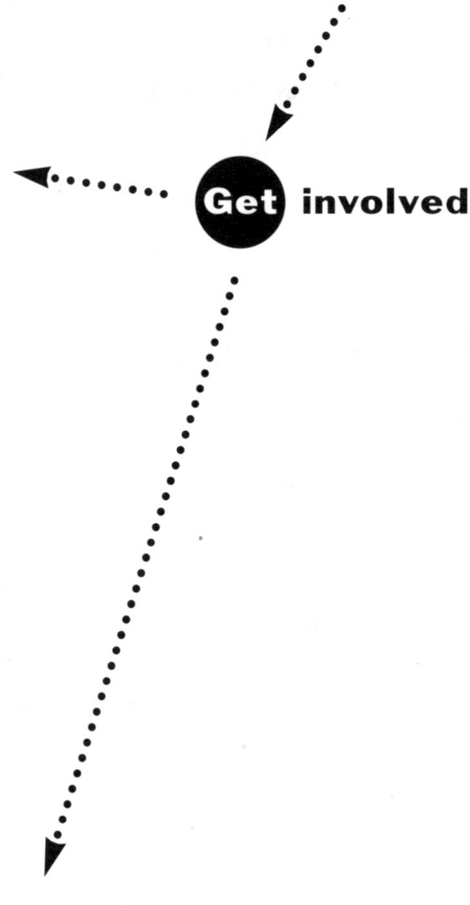

Students will follow your lead, so know where you are going. Come to class well-prepared so your time with the students will flow smoothly.

Materials: Bibles, index cards, marker, fitness video, picture of the White House and director's chair (or folding chair labeled "Director").

Before class: Write the following scenarios and questions on two index cards.

◊ *Group 1*

Your group has just been transported to a world where no one is in charge. No one rules over anyone else. There are no leaders.

♦ What are the drawbacks of living in this society?

♦ What are the dangers of living in this society?

♦ Do you think this kind of society could survive?

◊ *Group 2*

Your group has just been transported to a world where everyone is in charge of each other. Every person has a right to rule over everyone else.

♦ What are the drawbacks of living in this society?

♦ What are the dangers of living in this society?

♦ Do you think this kind of society could survive?

Leaders of the Pack

To start off today's lesson, I'm sending the class on a trip to another world. *(Divide the class into two groups. Send each group to opposite corners of the room.)* You have now been transported to worlds on opposite sides of the universe. *(Give each group an index card.)* Your card describes the unique features of your new world. Answer the questions on your card and be prepared to report your conclusions to me in three minutes. *(Give groups time to discuss, then ask them to share their answers with the rest of the class. Lead them to conclude that in a leaderless society, people are unorganized, have little purpose and can be left unnoticed or uncared for; in a leader-filled society, everyone would have his own goal or plan and want to see it accomplished, disregarding the needs of other people.)*

From the answers you came up with in your groups, it's easy to see that life without leaders would be pretty chaotic. Life with too many leaders and no followers would also spell disaster.

God knew the problems that could arise without leadership in His Church, so He came up with a plan for His followers. As the ultimate leader of His Church, He orchestrated events that showed the early believers why and how to choose leaders from among themselves. Let's turn to Acts to read about those events. *(Have students turn to Acts 6:1-7 in their Bibles. Assign one verse each to seven students and have them read the verses to the rest of the class.)*

Leadership: Part of God's plan for powerful ministry.

- ◆ **Why did the early Church need more leaders?** *To make sure the needs of the people were being met.*

- ◆ **What was the result of having the new leaders around?** *The Word of God reached more people. More people became believers.*

- ◆ **How do you think the selection of these seven leaders influenced the spreading of God's Word?** *The apostles were free to devote more time and energy to telling others about Jesus and less time worrying about the day-to-day situations in the church. The people in the church were helped. The seven men led in the areas they were given so the people they dealt with would be touched by His Word through them, etc.*

- ◆ **Why do we need leaders in our church?** *To care for us and help us care for others; to help get the word out about Jesus; to give oversight and direction.*

- ◆ **Why do we need leaders in general?** *To guide us; to help us grow as people; to give us direction; to keep us safe; to help us make decisions; etc.*

This passage of Scripture helps us understand the primary reasons for leadership in the Church Alive. God designed church leadership as a way of taking care of His children and spreading His Word so more people could know Him.

Leading the "God" Way

There are common traits that most leaders share, whether they are church leaders, government leaders or leaders of business. Let's see what those qualities are.

(Stack the video, picture and Bible on the director chair in front of the class. Identify the leader each object represents: Bible/pastor; video/exercise instructor; White House/President and chair/movie director.)

- ◆ **What leadership qualities would the instructor on the video, the President of the United States, the director of a movie and a pastor have in common?** *They work with people, communicate with others, offer guidance, motivate others, etc.*

A lot of people think a leader is a person who has been given a position or title and then starts to lead. For instance, a president would be voted into office and then his leading would begin, or a company would hire someone to be in charge of an area and they would begin leading in that area—the leadership qualities we just listed would begin to happen in their lives.

Do you think this would work? *No, a person has to show leadership skills in order to be chosen to lead.* Although all leaders share common traits, God's leaders have additional characteristics that are different from those of other leaders.

God's kind of leadership requires people who demonstrate godly traits and leadership *before* being given a position. **What did the Scripture from Acts say the leaders were already doing when they were chosen?** *They were good, full of wisdom and full of the Holy Spirit.* God's leaders already lead and care for people before they are given a title. Some of God's leaders never even have titles like "pastor" or "teacher," but they lead nonetheless.

Leadership: Part of God's plan for powerful ministry.

God wants His leaders to be caught in the act of leading even *before* they are given official responsibility. That's why the people in the verses in Acts 6 were able to agree on the seven men who were chosen to be leaders. *(Reread verses 3-6 to the class.)*

♦ **What did the apostles tell the other believers to look for in a leader?** *Men who are good, full of wisdom and full of the Spirit.*

♦ **What did the people think about the apostles' idea?** *They liked it.*

♦ **Why do you think those three characteristics are important for leadership in the Church?** *(Have students share.)*

♦ **How might those same characteristics be important for leadership in Club 56? in your classroom at school? in your home?**

In order to find the best leaders, all the people had to do was look at who was already demonstrating the godly traits needed in leadership. The seven men they chose were caught in the act of being leaders. The apostles agreed with the observations and officially placed the seven men in positions of leadership.

A Child Shall Lead Them—You!

Everyone in this room has an opportunity to be filled with the Spirit. We can all grow in wisdom, too, as we get closer to God. The Lord can also help us make right decisions and live good lives. I guess that means we have a room full of potential leaders!

♦ **What are some areas in our church where you could be a leader?**

♦ **What are some areas in your school and neighborhood where you could be a leader?**

Leadership qualities like the ones we read about in Acts don't just happen to a person. They are traits and qualities that are developed in a person through time and experiences. You have already gone through experiences that have developed these traits in your life. Every time you go against the crowd and do the right thing, encourage someone else to do the right thing or reach out to a person and think of their needs, you are continuing to develop those traits **and** you are becoming a leader—God's way.

Leading people to God through love, support and going the extra mile is God's plan for leaders. Any leadership that steers people away from God or encourages actions or attitudes which displease God is against His kind of leadership.

♦ **In what ways are you presently a leader with your friends?**

♦ **What leadership qualities do you admire the most in your leaders? teachers? parents? friends?**

♦ **What steps can you take to develop these traits in your own life?** *Spend more time with good leaders; ask God to help develop those things in me through the Holy Spirit; do the things He tells me to; etc.*

Remember that leaders lead—they don't take over. Allow students to discover solutions on their own. Their relationship with you will be strengthened when they see you respect their abilities.

Conclusion

To God, leadership is all about ministry—looking out for the needs of others. Remember what we read today? The whole reason more leaders were chosen in the early Church was to insure that all of God's people would be cared for. In contrast to the world's perspective of leadership, which focuses on giving a person power to rule and lead after being elected, God's plan for leadership focuses on serving others. It is a practice of the heart that has taken place before a title is given.

God wants to use you as a leader. You can make a difference in the lives of others and lead them to Jesus by caring for their needs. Live the life of a leader today, and watch what God does to recognize you. Let's talk to Him about it now.

Dear God, please help all of us to be able to recognize how we are leaders right now. In areas where we're leading people the wrong way—away from You—please convict us and we will stop. Help us to see where we are leading in Your way and influencing people to love and serve You, Lord. That's what we want to do. We give You permission to continue developing leadership qualities in each one of us. We want to be Your leaders in this class, our church and in every area of our lives.

Help us, too, Lord to respond correctly to the leadership You have given us in Club 56, our church and every area of our lives. Help us to love and support those people who are in leadership in our lives. In Jesus' name, amen.

Leadership: Part of God's plan for powerful ministry.

Materials: Bibles, string (or yarn), cups (large, Styrofoam) and scissors.

Before class: Punch a small hole in the bottom of the Styrofoam cups. Measure and cut 20-foot lengths of string. You will need one Styrofoam cup and one 20-foot length of string for each team.

Our Memory Verses today remind us that the early Church was told to choose seven good men to act as leaders. These men were to be full of both wisdom and the Holy Spirit. I am going to choose some leaders from among you to help with our game today. Choose leaders for each five- to seven-member team you will have. Allow the leaders to choose their teams.

With your team and your Bibles, look at and memorize the verses, Acts 6:3-4. You will need to know the verses when you play the game in a minute. Split the class into seven-member teams to memorize the verses. Give them three minutes to work on the verse.

Give each team a Styrofoam cup and a 20-foot length of string. Have each team pick two players to act as string holders. These students will each take an end of the string, running one end through the hole in the cup. They should pull

Acts 6:3-4

So, brothers, choose seven of your own men. They must be men who are good. They must be full of wisdom and full of the Spirit. We will put them in charge of this work. Then we can use all our time to pray and to teach the word of God.

If your classroom is not 20 feet long, cut the string in a length that will fit in the room, or do this activity outside.

the string taut between them. Have the rest of the team line up in relay fashion behind one of the string holders on one end. The open end of the cup must face the team and be touching the hand of the string holder.

Many times the Holy Spirit is represented as a mighty wind. Since the early leaders who were chosen were supposed to be full of the Holy Spirit, we are going to test you to see how much mighty wind you possess.

On the go signal, a player from each team will run up to the cup and say the first two words of the Memory Verses, then give one big blow on the cup to try to move it down the string. They must then run back and tag the next team member, who repeats the actions of the first, saying the next two words of the verses. Continue play until one team blows the cup to the other string holder.

1—Bible Study

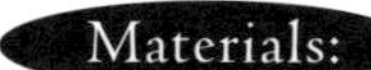

Materials: *Club 56 Activity Zone* page 8, Bibles and pencils.

We've heard a lot today about what it takes to be a leader and what leaders are supposed to do, but what is our responsibility as followers of the leaders in our lives? Let's check out an important verse in Hebrews which spells out pretty plainly what we are and are not supposed to do in response to our leaders.

Have the students turn to Hebrews 13:17 in their Bibles. Ask a volunteer to read the verse to the rest of the class. Distribute *Activity Zone* pages to the class.

So, there it is. We are supposed to obey our leaders and be under their authority. The verse says, "It will not help you to make their work hard." What do you think that means?

Think for a minute about different leaders in your life. *Parents, teachers, pastor, student council members, etc.* **Choose one and list the benefits (to you and him) of making his work easy and the downfalls of making his work hard.**

Have the students share the leader they chose and the things they wrote with the class. Together, come up with a list of the benefits of making a specific leader's job easy.

2—Cooking

Materials: 7-Up (in 1- or 2-liter containers), sherbet (any flavor), cups, napkins and ice cream scoop.

What is our Power Point today? *Leadership: Part of God's plan for powerful ministry.* **How many men from the early Church were selected to be leaders in the church?** *Seven.*

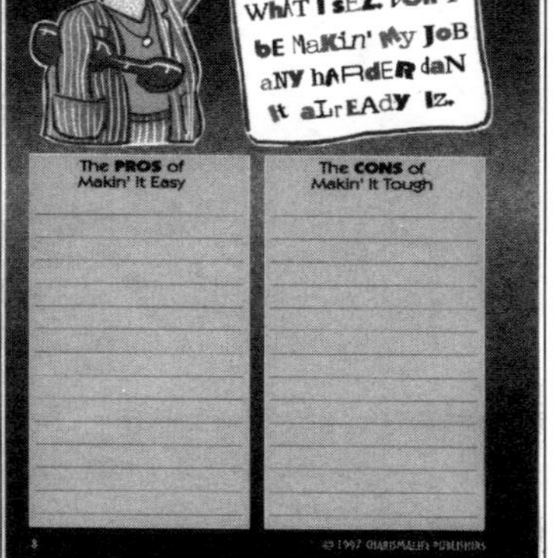

Activity Zone page 8

Since you have answered my questions so well, we're going to enjoy some "Litership" floats, celebrating also the "seven" who were filled "up" with wisdom and the Spirit of God.

Scoop some sherbet into the students' cups. Allow them to pour 7-Up into their cups. As they pour, they must say something they have learned about the need for leadership in the Church.

3—Individual Art

Materials: Paper (thin, white), crayons, cookie sheets (four, with sides), Jello (four 3-ounce boxes, different colors), hot water, measuring cups, spoon, vegetable oil, newspaper and hair dryer.

Note: Markers will not work in this project. Posters must be dried with a hair dryer.

We discussed the importance of leadership both during the time of Jesus and today. We also discussed some of the qualities that are seen in a good leader.

♦ How did the men in Acts 6 demonstrate their leadership qualities?

♦ What qualities can 5th and 6th graders develop that will make them good leaders?

During public elections, candidates create advertisements that attempt to convince the voters of their leadership skills. We are going to create marbleized leadership posters. On the poster, you will draw a picture of yourself. It can be a cartoon, profile or realistic portrait. Then, you will write a campaign motto about the qualities you already possess or are working on developing that make you a good leader. After you have finished your poster, you will have the opportunity to dip it in a mixture that will give it a marbleized effect.

Give each student a sheet of paper and crayons. While students are illustrating their posters, set up the gelatin mixtures as follows: First, lay out newspapers in two areas: one in which students can dry their posters and the other under the cookie sheets. Mix each box of Jello with 1 1/2 cups of hot water. Stir until the Jello is dissolved. Pour the four mixtures onto separate cookie sheets. Then, sprinkle a few drops of vegetable oil into each mixture. Stir with a spoon.

When the students are finished illustrating their posters, they can dip their papers into the Jello and oil. Students may wish to dip them in only one color or may chose to try a combination of colors. They can then place the posters on the newspaper while they dry them with a hair dryer. It will take about a minute to dry each paper. The leadership posters can be displayed for the class to view.

4—Outreach

Materials: *Club 56 Activity Zone* page 11, Bibles, envelopes, stamps and list of church leaders.

Before class: Compile a list of leaders in your church and their addresses. Include as many leaders as you have students. Include leaders in administrative, counseling, janitorial, lay pastor and music ministry positions. Write the name, address and position of each leader on individual strips of paper.

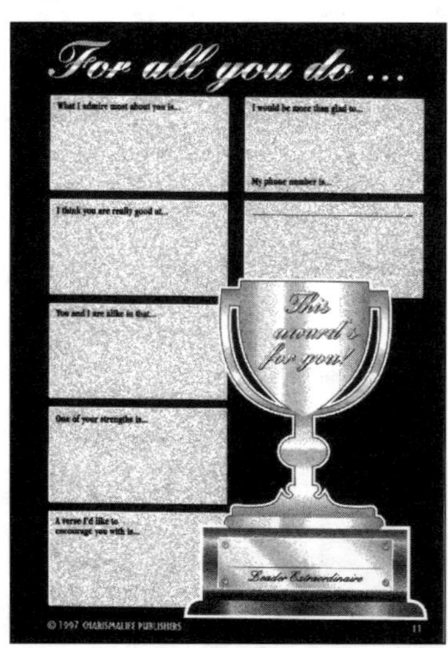

Activity Zone page 11

Rather than get frustrated with the student who is the ringleader of inappropriate behavior in the class, give him opportunities to exercise his leadership skills in a positive way. Get him on your team by giving him special responsibilities during class time.

Leadership: Part of God's plan for powerful ministry.

Our outreach projects usually are geared toward people outside of our church, which is why they are called "OUTreaches." Today, we are going to look for ways to reach out to the leaders in our church, who day in and day out find ways to give to us.

Distribute *Activity Zone* pages and name and address papers. Take a moment to think about the leader on your paper. If you do not know who the person is, ask the kids around you if they can tell you more about him. After you know a little bit about the person, fill in the spaces on your page to create a certificate of appreciation to encourage your leader. In the section of your paper that reads, "I would be more than glad to help you..." think of something you could do to help your leader. You could offer to babysit, mow his lawn or help clean his office. What are some other things you might be able to do for someone in leadership? Have students share ideas.

Write your phone number so he can call you and set up a time for you to follow through on your offer.

On the section that has no words, write another statement of your own choosing about the leader.

After students have completed their pages, have them pray together specifically for each leader. Have students address and put a stamp on their envelopes. Be sure to mail the certificates this week.

"The children in China just loved singing this song. They picked it up right away, even though it was in English," Mrs. Woods proclaimed proudly to the class.

"All she does is talk about China. If she thinks the children there are so smart and gifted, why doesn't she just go there and stay?" Riley whispered to Kelly, rolling her eyes.

"I know. It's like she's trying to make us feel guilty for being Americans or something," answered Kelly as quietly as she could. Between songs, the girls continued talking about their choir director, Mrs. Woods, who had recently returned from a six-month missions trip in China. The girls were tired of hearing her rave about the children she had met while she had been away.

"The next time she starts in again about how well-behaved and talented the kids are in **that** church, I'm gonna say something. I mean it, Kelly! I'm going to stand up in front of everyone and tell her to go back to China," Riley said with determination. Kelly knew Riley well enough to know she meant what she said.

"I don't know about that, Riley. I mean, she is our leader and all. Don't you think telling her off is a little out of line, considering what we talked about in Club 56 last week? Remember all that stuff we learned about leadership being from God?" Kelly asked nervously.

"It's not the same thing, Kelly. That was about pastors and big-time church leaders, not choir directors. Besides, you're the student president of the choir, and she doesn't seem to give you much respect. It'll be funny and get her quiet at the same time," Riley whispered.

"Don't, Riley. It's just not right. Just ignore what she says and sing the songs the way she wants us to," Kelly whispered, growing more nervous at the thought of what might happen if Riley followed through with her plan. *There's got to be a better way to do this,* she thought to herself.

"What are you two whispering about, Kelly?" Mrs. Woods asked. "As a leader in this group, I would think you would know to show a little more respect for your teacher and classmates. The children in China never would have dreamed of..."

Kelly didn't wait to hear Mrs. Woods finish her sentence. She stood to her feet and before she had a chance to think things through, said...

What happened next?

Divide the class into groups of two. Give them two minutes to decide what they think Kelly did. Have each group report their ending. Ask the following questions of the whole class, allowing students to answer.

♦ As a leader in the choir, what do you think are Kelly's responsibilities in this situation?

♦ What leadership skills do you think Kelly needs to get her through this situation?

♦ What would you do if you were in Kelly's position?

Not everyone is a born leader. When emphasizing the importance of leaders in God's family, be sure to mention the significance of helpers, encouragers and supporters. In doing this, no one in your class will feel left out.

Materials: Copies of *Club 56 Leader's Manual* Lesson 5 ACTS File Page page 61.

What is our Power Point today? *Leadership: Part of God's plan for powerful ministry.* In our church, the top person in leadership is (name your senior pastor). What are some things you like about our pastor? Allow students to share. Add things you admire about him.

This week you will be collecting data and inputting it in the ACTS company files. Your assignment is to ask as many people in our church as possible what quality they most admire in our pastor. List the various characteristics you accumulate on the computer screen on your page.

We will compare the lists next week to see what qualities people think are great in our pastor.

Be sure to bring your File Pages back with you next week so they can be added to your ACTS folders.

Leadership: Part of God's plan for powerful ministry.

ALIVE **C**HURCH **T**ECHNOLOGY **S**ERVICES

This week you will be collecting data and inputting it in the ACTS company files. Your assignment is to ask as many people as possible what quality they most admire in our pastor. List the various characteristics you accumulate on the computer screen.

ITEMS NEEDED FOR LESSON

❑ ACTS folders
❑ Lesson 5 ACTS File Pages

1—Creative Writing
❑ *Club 56 Activity Zone* page 13
❑ Pencils

2—Problem Solving
❑ Two copies of *Club 56 Leader's Manual* page 74
❑ Index cards
❑ Pencils

❑ Balloons
❑ Masking tape

❑ Bibles
❑ Chalkboard
❑ Chalk
❑ Index cards
❑ Pencils

3—Game
❑ Building materials (such as blocks, popsicle sticks, toothpicks, Styrofoam cups or empty toilet paper rolls—ten of each)

4—Music
❑ *Club 56 Activity Zone* page 14
❑ Pencils

❑ Bibles
❑ Butcher paper
❑ Construction paper
❑ Scissors
❑ Markers
❑ Glue (or tape)
❑ Masking tape

❑ None

❑ Copies of *Club 56 Leader's Manual* Lesson 6 ACTS File Page page 73

- -

SPECIAL NOTE

Before class, you will need to contact two students who are equally matched in their speaking abilities for More Activities 2. If you don't have two students who are capable, have two adults act as the lawyers.

My choices affect many people.

He fell on his knees and cried in a loud voice, "Lord, do not hold this sin against them!" After Stephen said this, he died. Saul agreed that the killing of Stephen was a good thing.

Acts 7:60–8:1

Acts 5:1-11; 6:5-15; 7–8:1

A. Strong Words

B. The Best Offense

C. Truth: Just Do It

D. What About Me?

IT'S TO DIE FOR

I knew I had arrived—the leadership of the summer day camp I had attended for a couple of years had asked me to be a junior counselor at the very mature age of 12. I felt privileged to assist the full-fledged counselors. I was especially excited about the one-night camping trip at the beach that always ended the day camp. It was an exciting time for both kids and counselors. This year it meant I got to stay up after the kids went to bed and have counselor fun.

After talking for a while, some of the counselors decided to take a walk. We walked down the beach and decided to stop for ice cream. It was late, though, and the ice cream stand was closed.

The older counselors decided to break into the snack bar and get some ice cream. I wasn't sure what to do. Inside, I was appalled. I resisted verbally, but after a few minutes I allowed them to talk me into it. It didn't seem like such a bad thing. There wouldn't be any harm, they assured me. There was no one around and the owners wouldn't miss a few ice cream bars.

They forced the small order window open. They needed someone little to climb in to retrieve the ice cream. This was going too far. My training and upbringing kicked in. "No," I responded quietly. "I can't do that." So, a petite adult counselor climbed in, opened the freezer and handed ice cream out to everyone, including me.

We were suddenly surrounded by police officers with guns. They had watched and listened to our whole escapade. The snack bars up and down the beach had continually been broken into, and this night they had staked out the ice cream stand we chose.

All the adults were arrested. I was too young to go to jail, but I was severely reprimanded. I was fired from the day camp. My parents were called. My younger brother, who was a camper, was sent home, unwelcome to attend the day camp in future years.

My actions affected not only me, but my parents, the kids at camp, the owners of the camp, my brother and the owners of that snack bar.

Be strong in sharing the truth of God's Word, so the kids will have what they need to resist in every situation.

Materials: ACTS folders and Lesson 5 ACTS File Pages.

What was our Power Point last week? *Leadership: Part of God's plan for powerful ministry.* Your assignment for Alive Church Technology Services this past week was to find out from different people the good qualities of our pastor. What did you find out for ACTS?

Have students share the comments from their research. Pray together for your pastor, both for today's service and for her life. Pray that she will continue to be alive in her relationship with God and the church.

Have students put their ACTS File Pages into their ACTS folders.

opening activity

Materials: Balloons and masking tape.

Before class: Make a start and finish line with masking tape.

Our Power Point today is *My choices affect many people.* Although we may not always be able to control what happens to us or the situations we may be in, how we respond to these situations is very important. To illustrate this we are going to have a relay.

Divide the class into two teams (or three, if it is a large class). Have each team line up at the start line. Give each student a balloon. Don't move chairs or tables out of the way for this relay.

The first person on each team is to partially blow up her balloon and then let it go. The next student in line moves to where the balloon landed, partially blows up another balloon, and then lets it go. The game will not go in a straight line. The first team to cross the finish line, or the team to get farthest after all relay team members have had a turn, wins.

♦ Did you enjoy this game?

♦ Why was it frustrating? Allow students to talk about the frustration of where the balloon goes and the difficulty of getting to the finish line.

Many things in our lives are like this relay. They don't always go in the direction we intend. How we choose to handle those frustrating situations is very important.

♦ How did the actions (attempts) of others affect your participation on the team?

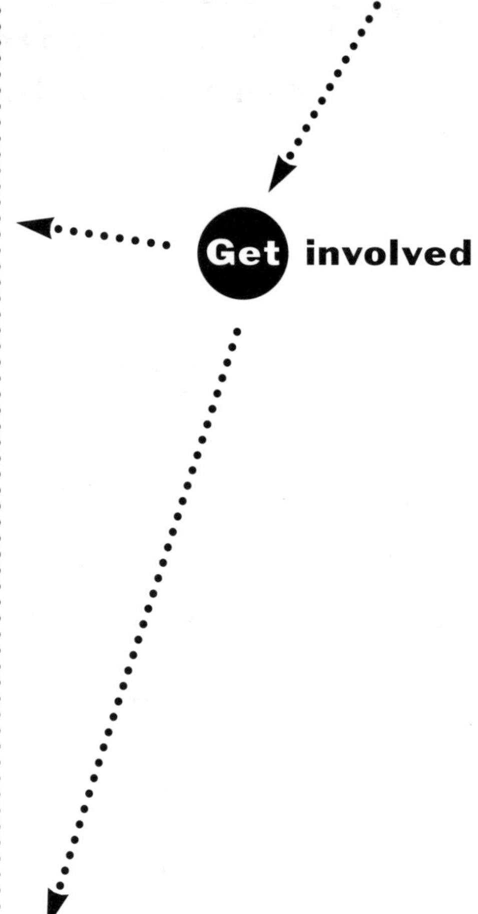

In order to try to keep an atmosphere of fun in what will become a frustrating game, keep encouraging the students as they race. If the balloon goes behind them, respond with "Keep it up, you'll get there eventually!"

My choices affect many people.

Pray before you lead this lesson that the students will be receptive to the message, that it will hit home in their spirits and they will feel confident in talking to the Lord about their decisions.

♦ What are some things your team could have done with your frustration? *Cheat by moving balloons, give up and not participate, etc.*

♦ Although those choices might have seemed OK at first, what would be the outcome of them?

Our Bible Lesson today is about how three people in the book of Acts handled choices and how their choices affected others. Remember, the book of Acts is about the Church Alive. In the Church Alive, our choices affect others.

Materials: Bibles, chalkboard, chalk, index cards and pencils.

Strong Words

As we continue our study of the book of Acts, let's begin by reviewing some characteristics of the Church Alive. **What can you remember from the past five lessons about the Church Alive?** Think about the Power Points. *(Write the answers on the chalkboard.) It's made up of people, not buildings. We are part of the Church Alive, just as the early Church was. The members of the Church Alive experience supernatural workings of God. People in the Church Alive know what they believe and believe what they know. People in leadership in the Church Alive have been given by God so powerful ministry can take place, etc.*

Today we will continue our study of the Church Alive by looking at a great man of God, Stephen. Last week we learned about how the apostles found other people who could be leaders in the church. Stephen was one of those leaders. Stephen had a good relationship with God. He also was a great help to the first church. Turn in your Bibles to Acts 6:5,8-10. *(Read aloud as the students follow along.)*

♦ **What were some characteristics of Stephen listed in these verses?** *He was a man with great faith, full of the Holy Spirit, richly blessed by God, had power from God to do miracles and signs, spoke with wisdom by the Holy Spirit and his words were strong—no one could argue with them.*

♦ **Who didn't care about those great characteristics?** *Some Jews who tried to argue with him.*

Since these Jews were so adamantly against Stephen, and yet couldn't argue with the wisdom with which he spoke, they had to find a different way to take care of him. Listen to what happened. *(Have a student read 6:11-15.)*

These people wanted Stephen to stop telling about Jesus. They wanted it so badly, they were willing to cheat and mislead other people to prove him wrong. Let's see what Stephen did.

Read Acts 7:1 out loud with me. "The high priest said to Stephen, 'Are these things true?'" **If this had happened to you, what would you say next?** *Defend yourself against the accusations; tell that those people were lying, etc.*

The Best Offense

Let's look at what Stephen actually did. His response to the high priest's question is 52 verses long, and we won't read all of it, but let's look at some of the highlights. As you and your group read your section of Scripture, listen for and be ready to share how Stephen defended himself to the high priest and the Jewish leaders and what he talked about to them. *(Split the class into four groups. Assign each group one of the following sections of Scripture to read: Acts 7:2-10, Acts 7:17-29, Acts 7:35-42 and Acts 7:51-53.)*

♦ Acts 7:2-10. *He didn't defend himself. He began telling the story of Abraham.* Instead of answering the charges by the Jews or defending himself, Stephen began to retell the stories of Abraham and Joseph, stories these men knew very well. What was Stephen thinking? Let's listen to what the second group found out.

♦ Acts 7:17-29. *He didn't defend himself. He told the story of Moses being born and trying to defend the Jews.* Again, in this section, Stephen told stories that the leaders knew well. Where was he going with this?

♦ Acts 7:35-42. *He didn't defend himself. He continued his storytelling and retold more parts of the story of Moses.* By this time, the high priest and Jewish leaders must have had really quizzical looks on their faces. Why was Stephen telling all these stories that were really familiar? Group 4 should have found out for us.

♦ Acts 7:51-53. *He didn't defend himself. He made accusations about the Jewish leaders.* He sums up all his stories in these three verses. Look at the last sentence of verse 51. *(Have someone read the sentence.)* **Now do you think the high priest and Jewish leaders knew what Stephen was trying to say with all the stories?** *Yes, he was telling them that they were not listening to God's prophets about Jesus. They were as bad as their fathers who killed the prophets.*

Stephen never did defend himself. Instead, he spoke to them by the Holy Spirit and told the truth. The truth, though, was not popular with those people. Let's look at the leaders' reaction to what Stephen said.

(Read to the class Acts 7:54–8:1.) Wow! What a price Stephen paid for making a choice to do what God was asking him to do—He was stoned to death. And yet, he made another choice in the midst of the stoning: Stephen asked God to forgive the leaders for what they were doing to him.

Both these choices affected someone we consider a great father of our faith, Paul. Did you notice in verses 58 and 8:1 that Saul (later named Paul) was there at the stoning? He even agreed that killing Stephen was the right thing to do. Of course, we know the rest of Saul's story—He became a mighty man of God himself. Stephen's choice to speak for God and to ask God to forgive the leaders influenced Saul.

Truth: Just Do It

Let's compare Stephen's death with two other deaths recorded in the book of Acts—the deaths of Ananias and Sapphira. *(Have one student find and read Acts 5:1-11 to the class.)*

Just as Stephen had choices to make, so Ananias and Sapphira were faced with some choices.

Each of your students may one day have to make an extreme sacrifice to choose to live for Christ. Pray for each of them today as you lead the class.

My choices affect many people.

- **What choices did they have?** *To sell their property or not; to give any or all the money from the sale to the church or not; to tell the truth or not, etc.*

- **What caused Ananias and Sapphira's death?** *They lied to the Holy Spirit. (Make certain your students understand that keeping back part of the money was not a sin, but lying about what they did was.)*

- **How did their choices affect them and other people?** *They died. The people were frightened.*

- **If there had been no serious consequences to Ananias and Sapphira's bad choices, what might have been the reaction to those who witnessed it?** *It would have appeared that dishonesty was rewarded and the Holy Spirit could be deceived.*

What About Me?

- **Who was affected by Ananias and Sapphira's choices?** *Ananias, Sapphira and all who heard about it.*

- **Who was affected by Stephen's choices?** *Stephen, Saul and all who witnessed it.*

- **Who is affected by your choices?** *You and all who hear about or witness them.*

(Pass out the index cards and pencils.)

Now we are going to try an exercise to see how our choices affect other people. Pretend this happened to you:

◊ While at school, you see two of your friends spray-paint graffiti on the outside of the gym. Later that day you are called to the principal's office. Your two friends are there. The principal says they told her you were there and could verify that they didn't do the spray painting. She asks for your verification. What do you do?

Without talking to anyone else, write the choice you would make in one or two sentences on one side of the index card. *(Give students two minutes to complete the assignment.)*

On the other side of the card, do these things:

◊ Make a list of those who will be affected by your response.

◊ Next to each person's name, write if she will be happy or upset by the effect your choice has on her.

(Collect the cards. Mix them up. Read who was affected and how. Have students discuss the choices.) Many of us thought of the principal, the two friends and some of our other friends who would be affected. **Who else might be affected?** *Ourselves, God, our families, people who hear about it later, etc.*

Just as Stephen, Ananias and Sapphira's choices affected many people around them, so the choices we make affect many people around us. Our choices also affect us! **How could the choice you made with this story affect you?**

When reading the index cards, try to keep the writing so only you can see it. Then, when placing the cards in their piles, place them face down. Always protect your students' anonymity so they can feel safe in their honesty.

Conclusion

Stephen received his power and strength from God. The Spirit worked through him and peoples' lives were changed. He made the choice to listen to and follow God, regardless of the cost to him.

The example of Ananias and Sapphira shows us a very different kind of situation and choice. They chose to lie to the apostles. Their choice had grave consequences for them.

The choices we make, big or small, affect many people. You face choices every day. Just as Stephen did, you can choose to follow God and do what He says. Whatever choices you make, remember: Your choices affect many people.

(Encourage the students to pray with one other person in the room. Have the groups of two pray for each other and the choices that will face them this week.)

 **Materials:** Bibles, butcher paper, construction paper, scissors, markers, masking tape and glue (or tape).

 **Before class:** Cut construction paper in half to make 4 1/2- by 6-inch rectangles. You will need 37 rectangles. Hang butcher paper on the wall.

Let's read our Memory Verses for today. Turn in your Bibles to Acts 7:60–8:1. Have a volunteer read the verses.

In order to help us remember the sacrifice Stephen made, we are going to make a large poster of the verses on the butcher paper. We'll hang it on the wall. That way, whenever we need encouragement to make good choices, we can look at the poster and remember that Stephen looked to the Lord for support and he made choices that affected many people.

There are 36 words and one reference. Split them among the students in your class. Have each student write one of the words of the verses on her paper. She can cut out the word, make designs in each letter, make "wacky" letter designs, etc.

When the students have finished, have them attach their words to the butcher paper in the appropriate places. The class should say the Memory Verses together several times.

Acts 7:60–8:1

He fell on his knees and cried in a loud voice, "Lord, do not hold this sin against them!" After Stephen said this, he died. Saul agreed that the killing of Stephen was a good thing.

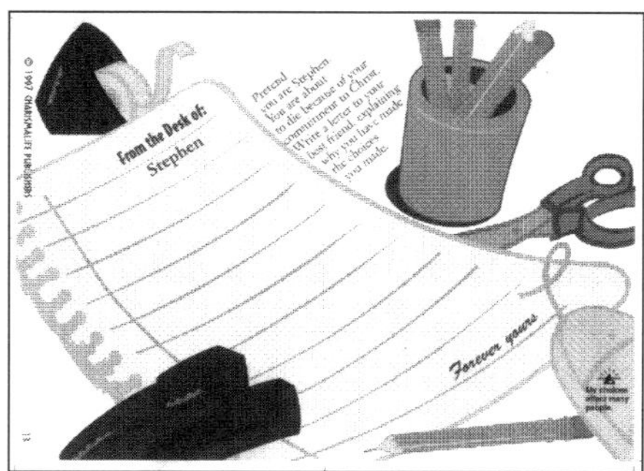

Activity Zone page 13

My choices affect many people.

1—Creative Writing

Materials: *Club 56 Activity Zone* page 13, and pencils.

The choices Stephen made affected many people. You have a chance now to have them affect even more people. Give students the *Activity Zone* pages.

Pretend you are Stephen and you have time before you die to write one letter. Write a letter to your best friend, explaining why you made the choices you have.

After the students are done with their letters, ask them to share them with the class.

2—Problem Solving

Materials: Two copies of *Club 56 Leader's Manual* page 74, index cards and pencils.

Before class: Give two students copies of the Defense and Prosecution final arguments. See Special Note on page 62.

Have any of you ever served on a jury? Of course not. You're too young. Today you're going to get your chance. You're going to hear the concluding arguments of two attorneys regarding the evidence about a defendant. One attorney is the defendant's lawyer, the other is the prosecution's.

It will be our job as a class to decide the fate of the defendant. You must act as though you have never heard this story. Decide the fate of the defendant based only on the statements made by the attorneys. Each of you can choose to let the man go free or you can decide to convict him. If together we find him guilty, then we must sentence him to be stoned. Listen carefully.

Give each student an index card and pencil. There will be no talking during the lawyers' presentations. You may make notes on one side of the card to help you remember what is said. At the end, you will write "guilty" or "innocent" on the other side of the card. Are you ready to hear the case?

Allow the defense first, then the prosecution to read their statements. Have both sides present their cases as written on the page. After the class has listened to the evidence, have each member cast her vote using the index cards. Collect and count the votes to decide the case. Announce what the outcome is—guilty or not guilty.

After the verdict has been read, allow the students to discuss why they voted the way they did. Ask them for reasons supporting their decision. Talk about what part(s) of the evidence convinced them.

3—Game

Materials: Building materials (such as blocks, popsicle sticks, toothpicks, Styrofoam cups or empty toilet paper rolls—ten of each).

Today we heard about the difficult choice Stephen made and the effects it had on others, particularly Saul. You are affected everyday by the choices of your parents and friends. Likewise, your choices affect those around you. Now we are going to play a game in which the choices made by you and your teammates affect each other.

Divide the students into groups of four. Ask each group to select one of the building materials available. Each group member should have ten of the building items.

Your goal is to see if your group can build a structure that will hold all of your building items without falling over. The rules of the game are as follows: First, the base of your building can include no more than four items. Second, your turns will go in a circle, so each group member places one item and then waits until all others in the group have had a turn. Finally, group members cannot talk to discuss strategies. You must remain silent. You will each make your own choice about where the next item should go without advice from your group.

After the groups have had a few tries at their constructions, discuss the following questions:

♦ How successful was your group at constructing a structure?

♦ Would your job have been easier if you could discuss strategies with the group?

♦ Did your choices in building affect the group? In what ways?

4—Music

Materials: *Club 56 Activity Zone* page 14 and pencils.

How many of you like to listen to contemporary Christian music? Today you get the opportunity to write your own musical lyrics. You don't need to make up a tune, but you may if you want to.

Give students their *Activity Zone* pages. Follow the directions on the page, and when you're done we'll all share our new songs about faith, either our own or Stephen's.

Competitive games are difficult for some students. If a student chooses not to participate, have her encourage the team by cheering for them.

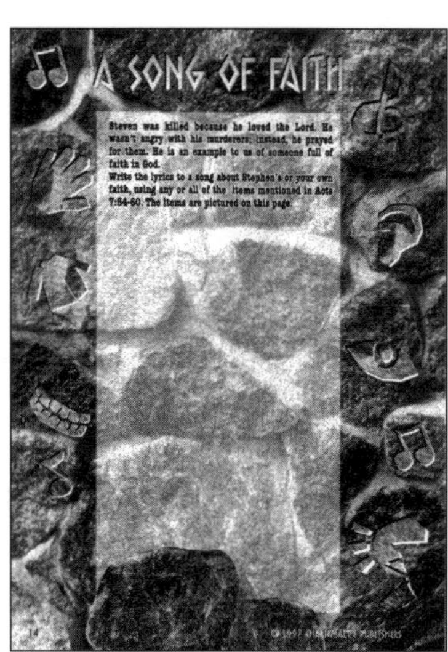

Activity Zone page 14

Steve grabbed the ball out of Jack's hand and laughed as he passed it to Wes. "Hey," he called to Jack, "did you get a new ball? This is great. You found one with air! Where'd you get it?"

They all laughed, but Steve noticed that Jack and Wes winked at each other and their laughs seemed a little nervous.

"Well, let's just say I found it," answered Jack. He and Wes grinned and ran off toward the hoop at the end of the school playground.

"Come on, Jack," Steve called as he followed them. "Where did you get the ball?"

Wes and Jack looked at each other. "OK, we'll tell you, but you can't pull one of those Christian things on us, OK?"

Steve nodded slowly, but then said, "What is that supposed to mean?"

"You know," said Jack, "how you always tell the truth, even when you know you're going to get in trouble. Well, this time you have to promise to keep your mouth shut!"

They were all silent for a minute. "Jack," said Wes, "I don't think this is very fair to Steve. He's our only friend who doesn't lie about things. It'd be pretty rotten if you made him lie!"

Steve was shocked that Wes and Jack had even noticed that he tried to never lie. Why would they care?

"I took it from the bag in Mr. Schaeffer's office," explained Jack. "He won't even miss it, and if he does, you just let me do the talking. Understand?" Jack tossed the ball to Steve who started shooting hoops.

"Uh oh," whispered Wes, "here comes Mr. Schaeffer!"

Jack stepped up in front of Steve, grabbed the ball and started bouncing it. "Hey Mr. Schaeffer, whatcha' doin'?"

The teacher looked at Jack and then at the ball Jack was casually bouncing. "I'm looking for a ball that looks just like that one. It was in the sack that I told you was off-limits. I didn't get a chance to imprint the school name on the items in that sack yet. Is that ball from the sack?"

He paused for a minute and then turned to Steve. "Steve? Where did you get that ball?"

Why does he have to ask me? Steve wondered. *Jack was right in front of him.* Now what was he going to do? He didn't want to lie, but how could he tell the truth?

What do you think Steve did?

Ask the entire class the following questions.

♦ List the choices Steve made. Which choice(s) put him in a position to get into trouble?

♦ What might make you think that Steve was suspicious of Jack and Wes? *He wasn't satisfied with their answers about the ball.*

♦ Why do you think the teacher chose to ask Steve instead of Jack about the ball?

♦ Why do you think Steve was surprised that people noticed he didn't lie?

Divide the students into small groups. Have each group decide on one positive and one negative ending for the story. Then ask which one they might actually do if faced with the same conflict.

My choices affect many people.

Materials: Copies of *Club 56 Leader's Manual* Lesson 6 ACTS File Page page 73.

What is our Power Point today? *My choices affect many people.*

Stephen, Ananias and Sapphira made choices in their lives that affected others. Almost every decision that is made affects people other than the person making the decision. Just ask around!

In fact, that is your Challenge this week. Alive Church Technology Services has assigned you to do research about choices. Poll the members of your family to find out about the choices they have made. Feel free to ask parents, brothers, sisters, grandparents, aunts, etc.

Ask each person you interview to think of one situation when her choice had a positive effect on others and a second situation when her choice had a negative effect. Describe two situations from your own life, too. Record your answers on the computer screen.

Be sure to bring your ACTS File Pages back with you next week.

My choices affect many people.

Club 56

SUGGESTED SCOPE & SEQUENCE

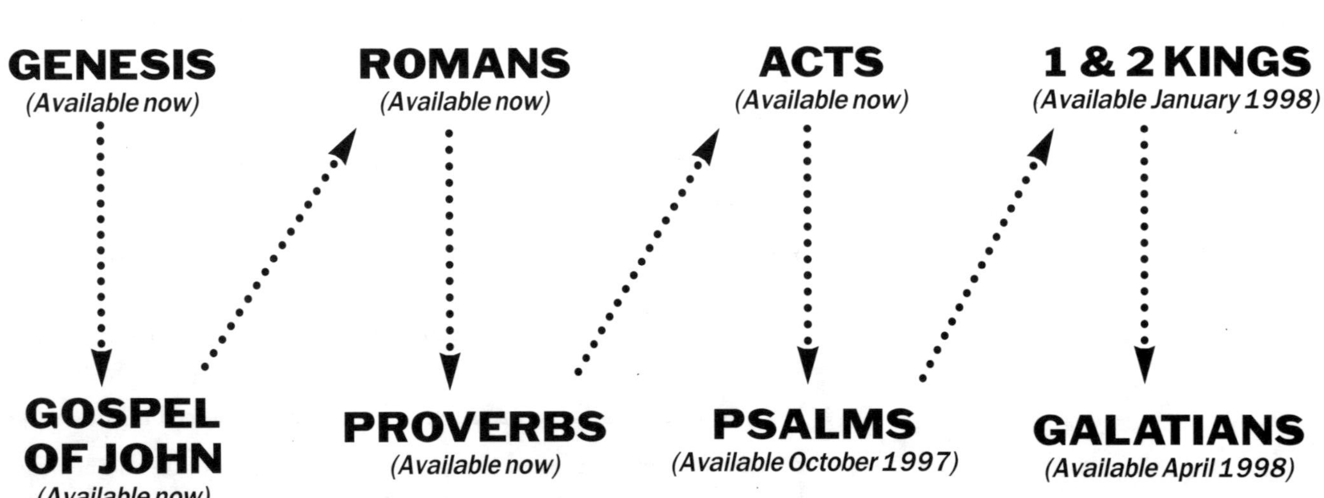

     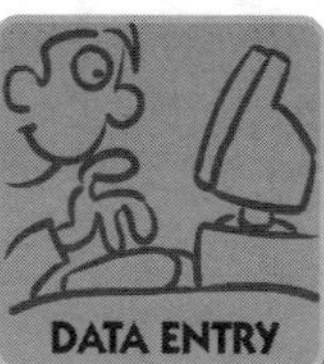

Alive Church Technology Services

Poll the members of your family about decisions they have made that have affected other people. Ask each person you interview to think of two situations, one in which her choice had a positive effect on others and one in which it had a negative effect. Describe two situations from your own life also. Write them on the back of this File Page. Record brief overviews of everyone's decisions on the computer screen.

You Decide: Guilty or Innocent?

Defense

I am here to give you the facts about my client, the defendant, Stephen. He has done nothing wrong and is totally innocent of the charges that have been brought against him. They are false.

Stephen is a good man of this city. We could fill this entire room with people who would testify to his excellent character. When Stephen became a believer in Christ, he was filled with the power of God. He was able to do many great miracles and signs because God was with him. Instead of doing wrong things, Stephen did what was good and right.

From the beginning, though, the Jewish leaders of this city were against him. They did not honor what he did or the God he served. Instead they tried to argue with him. However, they could not argue with Stephen because God gave him the words to say. The leaders only looked foolish when Stephen spoke. This made them so angry that they brought in witnesses who would lie about Stephen. These were not true witnesses, but instead were people who were paid to speak against him.

These witnesses said that Stephen had spoken against both the law of Moses and God. But that was an outright untruth. Right now we are in the process of interviewing these witnesses, and their stories are proving to be just that—stories, not the truth.

When Stephen went before the leaders and spoke to them, he simply reminded them that they, the leaders, didn't always obey the law of Moses. This made them very angry—but, hey, the truth hurts. Since when is speaking the truth wrong?

Stephen only spoke the words given to him by the Lord. As a matter of fact, while he was talking, the Lord revealed himself to Stephen. Stephen saw God as He was sitting on His throne in heaven—proof that Stephen was right in God's sight.

Please find my client innocent of the charges brought against him. Please find my client not guilty. Thank you.

Prosecution

Well, you have just heard the defense present their case of the so-called facts. I say "so-called" because they are not true.

Here is what really happened.

For quite a while the religious leaders of this city have been dealing with rebellious men who claim they are representing our great God. First there was Jesus and now His followers. They say they speak for God, but we know they don't. We know this because they speak against us, the representatives of God's law. How can that be?

We had witnesses come to us and testify against this man, Stephen. They accused him of speaking wrongly about God. When we brought Stephen before us, instead of answering the charges and defending himself, he lectured us on our history. It was quite upsetting. We already know all about our history. Who did he think he was to tell us? We know much more than he does. On top of that, he tried to turn everything around and put the blame on us.

The whole time Stephen was speaking, there was this strange glow on his face. If you ask me, it was because of his guilt. Guilty people always squirm and look weird when they are confronted with their own lies. What else could explain the strange, almost peaceful, look on his face? Strange, I say.

So there you have the facts: Witnesses who testified against Stephen and a definitely guilty look on his face.

Please put an end to this injustice! Cast a guilty vote against Stephen and end the lies he speaks.

COMPONENTS OF CLUB 56

Title Page

 **Power Point** — This is the main point you will emphasize throughout the Bible Lesson, activities and Challenge.

 **Memory Verse** — You and the students will learn this verse through a fun activity.

 **Lesson Scripture** — Read this section of Scripture to see what will be covered in the Bible Lesson.

 **Bible Lesson Outline** — This three- or four-point brief overview of the Bible Lesson helps you remember the points to go over as you teach.

 **Teacher Devotion** — This section shows how the Power Point can impact **your** life. Written from experiences in the writers' lives, these devotions will help you see clearly that this lesson is not only for 5th and 6th graders, but for you as well.

Extra Helps

 **Pastoring Tip** — Each lesson has pastoring tips to help you identify ways to minister to, care for and direct the 5th and 6th graders in their relationships with the Lord.

 **Teacher Help** — Short notes to give you further direction in activities for either large or small classes, to instruct you in practical wisdom about 5th and 6th graders or to point out safety considerations during an activity.

 **Power Point** — The Power Point is repeated throughout each lesson to help you remember the focus.

 **Memory Verse** — The Memory Verse appears in the column next to the Memory Verse Activity.

The Lesson

 **Challenge Review** — This section (in Lessons 2-13) will help reinforce the Power Point or Memory Verse from the week before, using the Challenge the students were given.

 **Opening Activity** — A fun, hands-on activity that will get the kids immediately involved in the focus of the Bible Lesson.

 **Bible Lesson** — The interactive Bible Lesson will cover three or four main points from the Lesson Scripture that will help the students understand how the Scripture applies to their lives.

 **Memory Verse Activity** — Fun activities for 5th and 6th graders that help the students memorize the Scripture and learn what it means for them.

 **More Activities** — Four additional fun activities that go along with the Power Point and Bible Lesson. There are a variety of activities so that every kind of learner can enjoy the activity time.

 **Living It Out** — A current-day, open-ended situation that the class will resolve together.

 **Challenge for the Week** — The Challenge helps bridge a student's home with your Sunday School class. Students work on the Challenge over the week and bring it back to discuss the following week.

 *Club 56 Activity Zone* — A full-color book that has two of the activities for each lesson. Order one for each student by calling CharismaLife Publishers, 1-800-451-4598.

ITEMS NEEDED FOR LESSON

- ❑ ACTS folders
- ❑ Lesson 6 ACTS File Pages

- ❑ Water pistols (two)
- ❑ Garbage bags (two, large)
- ❑ Shaving cream (one can)
- ❑ Shower caps (two)
- ❑ Tablecloths (plastic, or plastic sheeting)
- ❑ Scissors

- ❑ Bibles
- ❑ Index cards
- ❑ Pencils

- ❑ Bibles
- ❑ Star stickers
- ❑ Maps of the world (two)
- ❑ Map of the United States
- ❑ Maps of your city (two)
- ❑ Tape

- ❑ None

1—Individual Art

- ❑ *Club 56 Activity Zone* page 15
- ❑ Clip art book (or old newspapers)
- ❑ Pencils
- ❑ Church advertising page (from local newspaper)

2—Music

- ❑ Paper
- ❑ Pencils
- ❑ (Optional: Video camera and video cassette)

3—Outreach Project

- ❑ Paper
- ❑ Buckets
- ❑ Sponges
- ❑ Garbage bags
- ❑ Markers
- ❑ Vinegar
- ❑ Paper towels
- ❑ Scissors

4—Game

- ❑ *Club 56 Activity Zone* page 16
- ❑ Bibles
- ❑ Pencils

- ❑ Copies of *Club 56 Leader's Manual* Lesson 7 ACTS File Page page 87

SPECIAL NOTE

In the Memory Verse Activity, you will need several maps. Maps can be purchased at a low price through a secondhand store.

"New Kid in the Kingdom," an eight-page booklet that leads kids through the steps of salvation, is available from CharismaLife, 1-800-451-4598.

Walking with God: Risky living.

They were all worshiping the Lord and giving up eating. The Holy Spirit said to them, "Give Barnabas and Saul to me to do a special work. I have chosen them for it."

Acts 13:2

Acts 9:15-16; 13:2-3; 16:16-24; Matthew 28:18-20; Mark 16:15-18

A. Comfort Zone Christianity

B. Real Risks Equal Results

C. Calling All Christians

D. In the Meantime...

ME? A MISSIONARY?

It was a paper bank in the shape of a church building. I carefully carried it home from Sunday School. I had just one month to fill it up with extra pennies and nickels for the missionaries out there in China or Africa or some other remote place.

Slowly the little bank grew heavier. Contributions from Mom and Dad, aunts, uncles and friends helped to fill it to the brim. I would occasionally stop and shake it to hear the many coins rattle. I even remembered to pray occasionally for the missionaries and the children to whom they would tell the good news. With great pride, I carried my bank back to my Sunday School room at the end of the month. My missionary work was done. I had been dedicated to missions for the entire month.

That was about as far as my personal missionary experience went. I always saw the mission field as some far-off jungle in some remote spot to which I was not led to go.

As I have grown, I have learned that it is important to continue to understand and support missionaries and mission work on foreign soil. I have learned, too, that I have a mission field right in my own backyard.

While it is easy to see the need for an isolated village in China to hear the good news, we often miss the opportunity to tell the good news to the neighbors right out our front doors.

For 5th and 6th graders, learning to share their faith with those around them is a difficult assignment in the face of peer pressure and possible rejection. However, teaching kids to take steps to move out in their faith will help them grow.

Remember, the fields are ripe for the harvest—even if they are growing in our own neighborhood.

Materials: ACTS folders and Lesson 6 ACTS File Pages.

What was our Power Point last week? *My choices affect many people.*

Your Challenge from the Alive Church Technology Services was to do some research about choices. You were to ask family members about situations in which their choices had negative or positive results.

What did you find out? Have students share the stories they heard from their families. Continue to remind them about how their choices affect many people.

Have students put their File Pages in their ACTS folders.

Materials: Water pistols (two), garbage bags (two, large), shaving cream (one can), shower caps (two), tablecloths (plastic, or plastic sheeting) and scissors.

Before class: Fill water guns with water. Place the tablecloths under chairs.

Have you ever had the urge to do something that would be really risky? Maybe you would like to bungee jump or sky dive or really put yourself on the line by babysitting your neighbor's two-year-old.

♦ What is a risk you would be willing to take?

♦ Is there a risk that would be too great for you to attempt?

I am going to need two outrageously fearless volunteers who would be willing to take a risk and lead their team to victory. Do I have any such brave, bold and courageous students? Great. It's a daring job that I am going to ask you to do. You must be a leader for your team.

Divide the class into two teams. Add more teams if you have a large class. Cut a hole in the closed end of the garbage bag. Place this over your volunteers' heads and cover their clothes with it. Sit them in chairs at the front of the class. Cover the volunteers' heads with the shower caps. On top of the shower caps, squirt a large dollop of shaving cream so it looks like a giant Hershey's kiss. Line up the rest of the class in relay fashion in front of their leader's chair.

Now your job, team members, is to try to knock the shaving cream off your leader's head by squirting water at it with the squirt gun. Be careful, though.

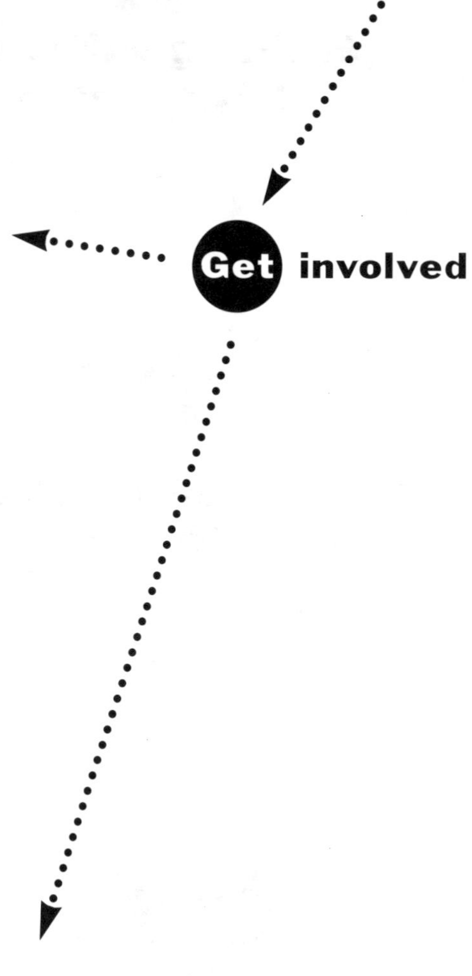

Watch for natural leaders in your class. Encourage them in their leadership, even as you encourage other kids in their giftings.

Your team must all get a chance, and you may not fill up the water gun again. Ready to begin? Let's go.

The first team to knock off the shaving cream is the victor.

That was a fun game. I appreciate the willingness of our brave volunteers who took a chance to risk themselves to be a leader to their teams.

Taking a risk can mean different things to each of us. Do you feel like you risk anything by being a Christian? What are some of the things you risk?

Our Power Point for today is: *Walking with God: Risky living.* Let's begin our lesson and see how walking with God can be a risky way to live.

Walking with God: Risky living.

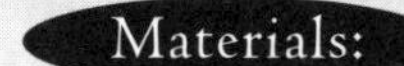

Materials: Bibles, index cards and pencils.

Comfort Zone Christianity

♦ Have you ever talked to anyone about God?

♦ Whom would you be willing to talk to about God?

♦ Would you ever talk to a stranger about salvation or Jesus?

♦ What kind of picture comes to your mind when you hear the word "missionary"?

It's easy to talk to other Christians about God. We know they will accept us and our beliefs. However, talking to others about God when we don't know them or don't know what they will think can be a risk. **What do you risk when you talk about God?** *(Allow students to answer.)* We put ourselves on the line when we declare our faith. Some people may accept us, but others will react negatively to what we say.

When we move out of our Christian circles, places where we know it is OK to talk about God, we move out of our comfort zones. We open ourselves up to rejection and possible ridicule—none of which is fun to experience.

So why should we do this? Why not just play it safe, keep it cool and not rock the boat? Maybe it will help if I read you some of the last recorded words that Jesus spoke. *(Read out loud or have a volunteer read the following.)*

◊ Matthew 28:18-20

◊ Mark 16:15-18

When we wonder why we should risk telling others about Jesus, we should remember Jesus' words. He spoke them to His disciples and today they apply to us. We need to move out of our comfort zones and walk with God wherever He leads us. That involves taking some risks.

Does that mean that we are all called to be missionaries? *Yes!* But everyone's mission field will be different. He might call you to go to Africa, or your mission field may be in your own backyard or a place in your own city that is foreign to you.

♦ Would you be willing to act as a missionary no matter where God called you to go?

♦ What would be the most difficult part of being a missionary?

Real Risks Equal Results

We have come up with some examples of the risks we might face when we share our faith. Let's look at some of the things that happened to one of the first missionaries of the early church—Paul.

(Ask for a volunteer to read Acts 16:16-24 out loud to the class.)

♦ What were some of the consequences Paul and Silas faced for telling about God?

♦ Do you think missionaries today face the same kind of risks?

♦ What would be harder for you to take: public humiliation like being made fun of at school, or physical punishment like what Paul and Silas faced?

♦ In what ways would it be harder to tell others about Jesus in a foreign country than here? In what ways might it be easier?

In the United States, we don't have to worry much about being thrown in jail for talking about our relationship with God. We are protected by the Constitution. It says we have the right to freedom of religion. However, more and more, it is becoming commonplace to put down people who hold Christian values. **Can you think of positive or negative examples of Christians on television or in the movies?** Many public places now restrict your ability to pray or read your Bible.

♦ Are you allowed to pray or read your Bible at school?

♦ Do you think this should be a right you have?

♦ Would you use this right if you had it?

Though there are some negative consequences to sharing your faith in our country, there is much more overt persecution in other countries. China and parts of Africa and eastern Europe all can be dangerous places for missionaries—places where missionaries risk their lives to spread the news of Jesus Christ.

Calling All Christians

Knowing that missionaries face many challenges as well as difficult situations might stop many people from wanting to become missionaries. **What would be some of the reasons someone might want to be a foreign missionary? How did Paul decide?** Let's take a look back into the book of Acts to find out.

(Have a volunteer read the following verses out loud to the rest of the class.)

◊ Acts 9:15-16

◊ Acts 13:2-3

♦ Who chose Paul to spread God's message?

To make this lesson more personal to the class, you might want to bring in pictures or letters of the missionaries that your church supports, and share about them during this time.

Walking with God: Risky living.

◆ What is something you could do to help determine if you are called to the mission field?

◆ How do you know when you have heard the Holy Spirit's direction?

Though all us of should be ready to share salvation, and therefore be missionaries, some of us may be called to a foreign mission. God may have plans for you to tell about Him to people who have no knowledge of Him. To find out what God has for us, we need to ask Him. If we pray and fast just as Paul and Silas did, God will also direct us in the purposes He created us for.

(Hand out the index cards and pencils.) OK, that all sounds good, but just imagine for a moment that you are a missionary in a foreign land. The country you are in is against the message of Christianity. As a matter of fact, you had to be smuggled in across the border. While you are sharing the good news with someone, you are stopped by a group of guards. They arrest you for your "subversive" activities. After a quick hearing, you are sentenced to death by a firing squad. As they line you up against the wall, a mysterious man enters the courtyard. He is obviously a man of importance. He approaches you and looks directly into your eyes. He speaks and tells you that you have exactly one minute, no more or no less, to convince him that all you say is true. **What would you say?** You have one minute to write it down on your index card. Remember, your life depends on your answer.

(Time the students for one minute. After the time is up, have each one share what he wrote for an answer.)

◆ Do you think your answer would convince the man?

◆ Is your answer good enough to save your life?

That would be a tough situation to face. If you were ever in a situation like that, you could trust God. He has promised to give you the right words to speak when the need arises.

In the Meantime...

So what do we do right now? **What are some of the things that 5th and 6th graders can do to share the good news?** *(Brainstorm with the class about some ways that they could help missionaries, some realistic ways to share their faith with friends or relatives and ways they are learning to trust God so if and when they face a situation such as the one they wrote about, their trust will be in Him.) Some possible ideas: Write letters to missionaries your church supports. Raise money for missionaries by setting up and running an espresso bar for church members before and after church, holding a car or windshield wash, etc. Plan a fun night where each person brings a non-Christian friend, use the booklet mentioned in the Special Note for themselves or with unsaved friends, etc. Encourage each other to grow in their relationship with God by trusting Him.*

There are many things we can do. We are really only limited by the boundaries we set up. It is easy to let ourselves off the hook by thinking we are too young or somebody else will do it, but if everyone thinks that way, nothing will ever get done. Today, we will be doing an outreach project to our neighborhood. We will be washing windshields on cars so we can be a blessing to our neighbors. This is one small way we can begin to be missionaries right around us.

Outside activities are an excellent way to encourage growth, both individually and as a class. Students also get to see how faith works outside of the classroom.

Conclusion

Now what comes to mind when you hear the word "missionary"? Sometimes God calls us out of our comfort zones and asks us to take some risks for Him. When we step out to tell others about our faith, we put ourselves on the line and experience some possible risks. With those risks also come satisfying rewards. Leading someone to Christ is one of the greatest gifts that the Lord allows us to participate in. Walking with God is not just risky, it is rich.

Let's pray and ask God to help us in these things this week. Father, we want to be brave children of Yours who risk ourselves for You and what You want on earth. Please help us this week to grow in our trust of You. Put situations in each of our lives that help us depend on You. Give us people who need to hear about Your love for them. And, Lord, give us the boldness to share with them. We love You, and want to not just talk about You here in Club 56, but to live with You all through our days this week. God, if part of Your plan is for one or more of us to one day share about You in a foreign country, help us to be sensitive to Your call. In Jesus' name, amen.

Walking with God: Risky living.

Materials: Bibles, star stickers, maps of the world (two), map of the United States, maps of your city (two) and tape.

Before class: Tape one of the world maps on the wall for students to see. On the map, place stars in locations of missionaries supported by your church. On the bottom of the map, write the Memory Verse.

In our Memory Verse, we learn that God set apart Saul and Barnabas to do a very special work. Let's take a few minutes to memorize the verse.

Give students time to look up the verse in their Bibles and memorize it alone or with a partner. Then, ask for volunteers to recite the verse.

Each one of us is called by God to do something special with our lives. Someday, we might have the chance to serve as foreign missionaries. On this world map, you can see stars that show where some of our church's missionaries live.

Draw the students' attention to different areas on the map. Discuss some of the obstacles the missionaries might face in the various countries (for example, climate, language barrier, other religions, different cultures, civil wars, etc.).

Many of us will never go overseas to serve as missionaries. Yet the Bible tells us that it is still our job to be missionaries by being witnesses for Him wherever we are.

♦ How can we be missionaries without going overseas?

♦ To whom could you minister in your own family? in your city? in our state? in our country?

Acts 13:2

They were all worshiping the Lord and giving up eating. The Holy Spirit said to them, "Give Barnabas and Saul to me to do a special work. I have chosen them for it.

Divide students into four groups. Ask each group to choose one of the maps. Give each group star stickers and have each student choose two places in which he would like to serve as a missionary. They can mark their choices with the star stickers. Give the students time to decide and discuss their choices. Finally, ask students to share their choices and discuss the following questions:

♦ Why did you choose these locations?

♦ What difficulties might you face if you were a missionary in your chosen area?

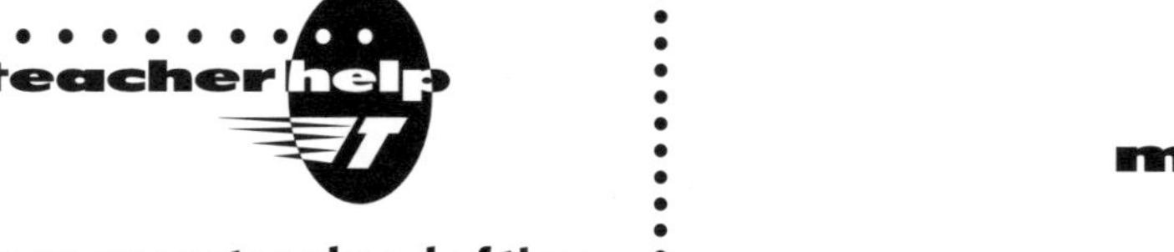

Talk to your pastor ahead of time about including some of the ads in your church bulletin or in advertising for the church. The kids will do a great job if they know that their work has a purpose and might be used.

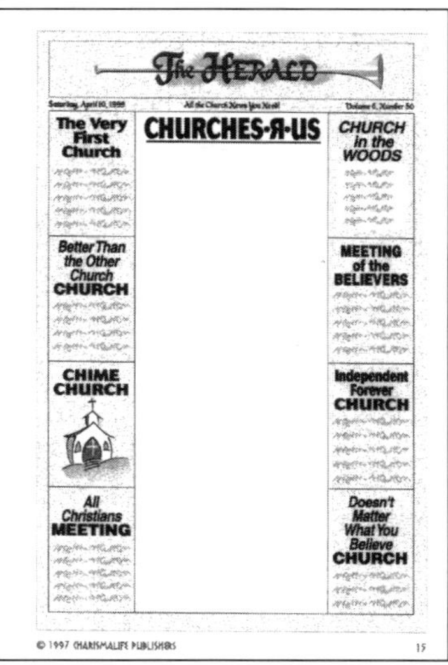

Activity Zone page 15

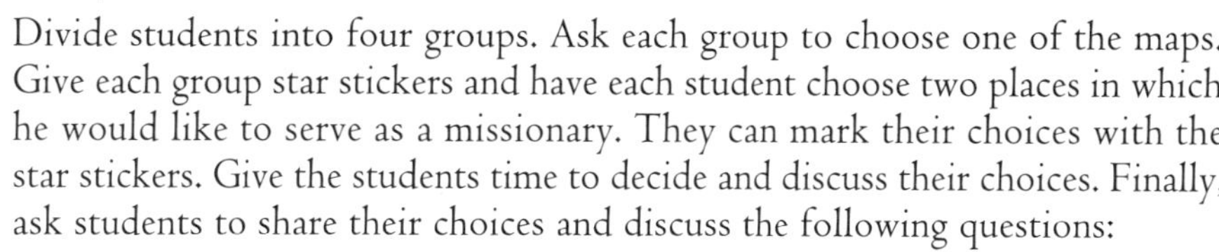

1—Individual Art

Materials: *Club 56 Activity Zone* page 15, clip art book (or old newspapers), pencils and church advertising page (from local newspaper).

Hold up or display the local church advertising page from the newspaper. **This is a newspaper page where churches place ads to tell people about their church. As you can tell by looking, there are many different approaches that individual churches use to catch your eye and tell you about themselves.**

♦ What ad do you find appeals to you the most?

♦ Which ads show that their churches are "alive"?

♦ What information do you think is important to include in an ad about your church?

♦ How could you create an ad that would attract kids to Club 56?

Each of you is going to design an advertisement that might be submitted to a newspaper that would tell anyone looking at it about Club 56 and our Church Alive. Think about what kind of print or lettering you would want to use. Also decide if you would want to include any pictures or logos.

Distribute the *Activity Zone* page to the students. Make the clip art book available for ideas. When everyone has completed his ad, have him share it with the class.

2—Music

Materials: Paper and pencils. (Optional: Video camera and video cassette.)

Have the students form groups of three or four. **You are a contemporary music group working for an ad agency. The ad agency has hired you to make a commercial for missionaries. Your commercial needs to get people to pray for and support missionary work in other countries. It needs a fun little song with words** that will help people remember it. With your group, you have five minutes to plan the commercial, think of a tune and words and practice to be ready to present it to the class.

Have the groups perform their commercials. If you have a video camera, record the commercials and make a copy to send to the missionaries from your church.

♦ How do you think our church family would respond to our commercials?

♦ What do you think the missionaries from our church would think about our commercials?

♦ Do you think that our missionaries could use some "commercial" support?

3—Outreach project

Materials: Paper, markers, buckets, vinegar, sponges, paper towels, garbage bags and scissors.

Before class: Cut paper into 5 1/2- by 4-inch pieces.

One way we can act as missionaries is to show our love to the people around us. We can do that by putting our love into action. Today we are going to go out in the neighborhood around our church, as well as the church parking lot, and wash the windshields on cars. We can also help to clean up the neighborhood by picking up any garbage we see along the way.

Before we go, though, we want to make small signs that tell why we washed the windshields. On each piece of paper, we need to write, "Your windshield washed by the kids of Club 56 at _(name of your church)_. Jesus loves you!" Have students write the two sentences on all the papers.

Before leaving the church, fill the buckets half full with warm water. To this, add a cup of vinegar. Take sponges, paper towels and garbage bags with you. Have someone carry the papers to put on the windshields when they are cleaned.

Students who want to protect their clothes should cut a hole in the finished end and on the sides of a garbage sack. The sack can then be slipped over their heads.

As you walk through the neighborhood, have students ask people if they may wash their car's windshield. Tell them that this is a free service you are doing for the entire neighborhood. When students finish and the windshield is dry, have them leave the note under the windshield wiper or hand it to the owner.

4—Game

Materials: _Club 56 Activity Zone_ page 16, Bibles and pencils.

Hand out the _Activity Zone_ page. Students may work alone or in pairs. **Paul sent you some postcards from different cities. Use the clues to find the city names and solve the crossword puzzle. Read the Bible verses to find out why the bold words in each clue are there. Be ready to share your answers with the class.**

When the class is done, have everyone share why the bold words are in the clue.

♦ What does the word have to do with the things that happened in the verses you read?

♦ Can you think of other clues that could be given about the same city or things that happened?

Walking with God: Risky living.

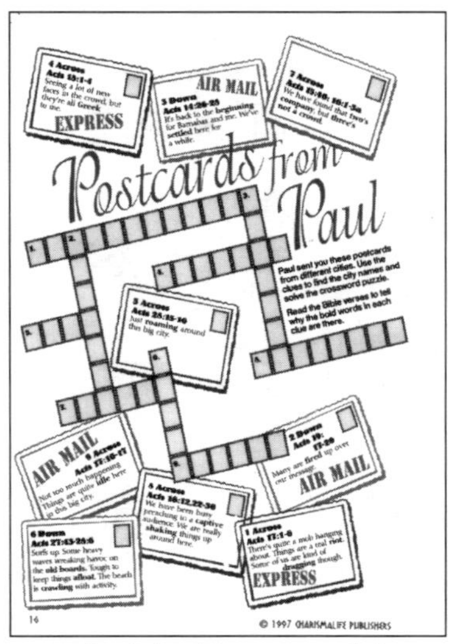

Activity Zone page 16

Answers:	
<u>Across</u>	<u>Down</u>
1. Thessalonica	2. Ephesus
4. Corinth	3. Antioch
5. Rome	6. Malta
7. Lystra	
8. Philippi	

Use Living It Out stories and the discussion afterwards to see how your students think and behave in real life. Allow the Holy Spirit to remind you of these things during the week so you can pray for each student.

Risa and Janny watched as the people took away their beloved possessions. "I didn't know that a garage sale could hurt so much!" said Risa.

"Maybe you feel bad because we don't get to keep any of the money from this sale," said Janny. "I think," she continued, "that they should at least let us have some of it because we worked so hard!"

Risa nodded and watched as her mother helped the man put her old doll-house in his car. "I know what you mean, but this is all for missions. Kids in Romania will get to have clothes and food because of this sale."

Risa wished that she were as excited about it as the rest of her family. Her parents had organized this church garage sale, and everyone had just assumed that she agreed with them.

"Risa, will you help this lady pack books into her bag? Thanks, honey. We sure are making a lot of money for missions today." Her mother hurried off to help another customer.

"Janny," asked Risa when she finished packing books for the customer, "why are we doing this?"

Janny looked at her blankly. "Because our parents told us to. Why?"

Risa looked at her friend and spoke hesitantly. "Well, if this is for missions, why don't we ask to keep part of the money for a VCR for the 5th and 6th grade room?"

Janny gasped and turned to her friend. "Risa, that's perfect! And we could use it for helping others. Like when kids bring their friends that aren't Christians. That's a ministry, isn't it?"

Risa quickly agreed, "Remember, part of the class mission statement is to be prepared to help others in any way we can. This will be great for our class, too. We won't have to wait for the youth group before we can watch a movie. And we can even watch missionary films! We are going to need to get our parents to go along with this idea."

That evening Risa presented her idea to her parents. When she was finished, her mother just looked at her for a minute before she answered.

"I have a real problem with this idea, Risa. Why don't you prepare a statement presenting each side of the argument and present it to the class and let them vote?" That seemed like a great idea to Risa.

What do you think the class decided?

Divide the class into two groups. Have one group present sending all the money to Romania, and the other present purchasing a VCR for the classroom with some of the money. After they present their ideas, ask the class to vote for what they would do.

Materials: Copies of *Club 56 Leader's Manual* Lesson 7 ACTS File Page page 87.

With all this talk about missions, Alive Church Technology Services wants to conduct an official survey of the people in this church to determine how many missionaries the average attendee can name. Your Challenge this week is to talk to as many people in our church as you can. Ask them to name missionaries and the countries where they minister or ministered. For each missionary's name you collect, give yourself a point. For every different country you collect, give yourself two points. List the names and corresponding countries on your computer screen and tally your points in the mouse. We will see who collected the most points.

Be sure to bring your File Pages back with you next week.

Walking with God: Risky living.

TIME TO REORDER

It's time to order *Club 56* for next quarter. To make sure your order gets filled promptly and to qualify for any special discounts or offers, place your order NOW!

Please check with your CE Director or call your CharismaLife Christian Education Consultant at

1-800-451-4598

Alive Church Technology Services

Tally the number of missionaries the people in your church can identify. Each name earns one point. No points are earned for duplicate names. If the country where the missionary ministers (or ministered) is identified, add another two points. No points are earned for duplicate countries. The missionaries identified may be supported by our church or may be acquaintances of church members. Names of well-known missionaries in history are also acceptable. Write the missionaries' names and countries on your computer screen. Total your points in the mouse.

ITEMS NEEDED FOR LESSON

❏ ACTS folders
❏ Lesson 7 ACTS File Pages

❏ Masking tape
❏ Balloons
❏ Peanuts (in the shell)

❏ Bibles
❏ Light bulb
❏ Lamp
❏ Kleenex
❏ Magnifying glass
❏ Metal container (shallow)

❏ Wallpaper samples (or construction paper)
❏ Permanent markers
❏ Pencils
❏ Butcher paper
❏ Scissors
❏ Glue
❏ Cardboard
❏ Tape

❏ Copies of Living It Out (story only)
❏ Pencils (red)

1—Bible Study

❏ *Club 56 Activity Zone* page 17
❏ Bibles
❏ Pencils

2—Game

❏ Cotton balls
❏ Vaseline
❏ Buckets (two)
❏ Wipes

3—Problem Solving

❏ None

4—Drama

❏ *Club 56 Activity Zone* page 18
❏ Lunch boxes
❏ Newspaper
❏ Camera
❏ Photographs
❏ Pillows
❏ Chair

❏ Copies of *Club 56 Leader's Manual* Lesson 8 ACTS File Page page 99

. . . .

SPECIAL NOTE

Be aware that spiritual warfare is likely to happen as you prepare and teach this lesson. Satan truly is alive and wants to convince the kids in your class that God is not alive, or if He is that He has only a minimal effect on their world. Pray now for God's covering as you prepare and as you teach. Practice the warfare you will teach as you prepare: 1. Identify the source of the power. 2. Be **with** God. 3. Listen to Him and obey what He says. 4. Watch the results.

Wallpaper is ideal to use for the Memory Verse Activity because of the various designs, colors, and textures. Most wallpaper stores have discontinued sample books that they are happy to give away or sell at a very modest price.

Nothing or no one is more powerful than God.

All the people in Ephesus, Jews and Greeks, learned about this. They were filled with fear. And the people gave great honor to the Lord Jesus.

Acts 19:17

Acts 13:6-12; 14:8-18

A. Power Displays

B. Power for What?

C. God's Power for Today

D. Dealing a Death Blow to Satan

WHAT'S YOUR POWER SOURCE?

She couldn't believe it. The van had broken down again. This time Cindy was stuck on the side of a freeway. There had been so much trouble lately with finances, auto problems and repairs on the house, not to mention the emotional toll the troubles were causing each member of the family. Did God see? Did He care that she was 15 miles from home with no transportation? Did He understand that she couldn't handle one more thing?

As Cindy related the situation to me, she shared that a friend stopped and helped her get to a telephone. They talked, and the friend's words became the encouragement she needed from God right then. God Himself had sent an angel of mercy to help in this crisis.

Several days later, as she was driving alone on the same stretch of freeway, God spoke clearly to her. "You have promised to walk with Me all your life. I have promised you that I will always take care of you. What is happening is no mistake. Trust in Me." Although very little of the circumstances had changed, Cindy was instantly changed inside.

There are many powerful things that happen to us. The lasting power of God's love and care for us is the one thing that will survive all others. Cindy didn't need to have her finances fixed, her auto repaired or her house completed. She needed (and needs) God's everlasting presence in her life. She needed the power of His love to make it through life. God would give her direction for each of the difficulties she faced, and each would eventually be resolved. More important, He gave her His presence and support in the midst of every part of her life.

As you teach this lesson today, present the power of God's lasting and complete love for each student in your class. When they are touched by His love deep inside, they will be changed forever, regardless of the circumstances around them.

 ACTS folders and Lesson 7 ACTS File Pages.

What was our Power Point last week? *Walking with God: Risky living.* **Your Challenge was to have people in our church name missionaries and the countries where they minister or ministered. You gave yourself a point for every name and two points for every country. How many points did you get?** Have students share the number of points, then who and where the missionaries are or were.

♦ **Why might it be important to know missionaries' names and countries?**
To pray for them; to recognize if we hear or read about the country in the news, etc.

Let's pray right now for each of the missionaries we have listed. Have each student lead in prayer for the missionaries on her File Page. Encourage students to thank God for each missionary, as well as pray for her protection, her family, her ministry, her finances, etc.

 Masking tape, balloons and peanuts (in the shell).

 Make a starting and ending line for the relay with masking tape

How powerful are you? Encourage students to talk about different ways they are powerful, such as physical strength, mental power in learning, influence power over friends, etc.

Divide the class into two teams. **Today we're going to participate in a relay to help us see which team has more *breath* power.** Give each member of the teams a balloon. Each team should have one peanut.

Put your team's peanut on the starting line. All your team members should blow up their balloons. The first person in line will release her balloon's air toward the peanut. When her balloon is empty, the second person will do the same. The goal is to get your team's peanut to cross the finish line before the other team's. When you go to the back of your team's line, blow up your balloon again so you are ready to repeat the game. We will continue the game until one team has blown their peanut over the ending line.

Play the game, then gather the class together.

Get involved

Nothing or no one is more powerful than God.

Don't just read verses in the Bible. Always be sure students understand what a verse says and means before moving on to another verse or point in the lesson.

Did you have fun showing your team's breath power? Today we're going to talk about the great power of the universe: God's power. His power is greater than either team's breath power, of course, as well as any other power that exists. Our Power Point today is—*Nothing or no one is more powerful than God.*

Materials: Bibles, light bulb, lamp, magnifying glass, Kleenex and metal container (shallow).

Before class: Crumple Kleenex and put it and the magnifying glass in the metal container.

Power Displays

Name some people who have supernatural powers. *God and Satan. (Students may name fictitious characters such as Superman or people who are psychics, fortune-tellers, witches, etc.)* **What does the word "supernatural" mean?** *Something that is beyond natural or out of the ordinary.* Supernatural is not only about spooky or weird stuff, it is about things God does that are miraculous. Let's look in Acts 13:6-12 and see how two supernatural powers were at work during Paul and Barnabas' ministry. *(Have a volunteer read the verses. Stop her after each verse, asking kids to identify the main point of each. The main points are listed below.)*

- ◊ Verse 6—Paul and Barnabas met a magician, Bar-Jesus (Elymas in Greek).
- ◊ Verse 7—Elymas was a good friend of Sergius, the governor. Sergius wanted to hear about God from Paul and Barnabas.
- ◊ Verse 8—Elymas didn't want the governor to believe in God.
- ◊ Verse 9—Paul was full of God.
- ◊ Verse 10—Paul identified that Elymas' power came from Satan.
- ◊ Verse 11—Paul told Elymas what God was going to do to him. What Paul said happened. Elymas went blind.
- ◊ Verse 12—The governor believed in God because of this.

We see some amazing uses of power in this section of Scripture!

- ♦ **Which details show God's power?** *Paul had discernment with Elymas and spoke the truth about him. God blinded Elymas as a sign to Sergius that God is powerful.*
- ♦ **What things did Elymas do that showed Satan's power?** *He tried to stop the governor from believing in Jesus. He was full of evil tricks and lies. He changed the Lord's truth.*

♦ **What happened to his power?** *It was ineffective. It did not have the effect it was meant to.*

God's power is always greater than Satan's. It might seem like Satan is winning and his power is great, but God is always greater. God created Satan. Satan is a creation, not a god. He has only the power that was given to him. In just a minute, we'll look at what power he actually has on earth. Right now, though, let's look at one more power story from Acts.

(Split the class into three groups. Assign each group one of the following passages to read. They should be ready to tell the class what their section of Scripture says and means. Acts 14:8-10; 11-13; 14-18.)

♦ **When was God's power used?** *In the healing of the crippled man.*

♦ **How do we know Satan's power was active in the lives of the people?** *He confused the people. The people thought Paul and Barnabas were powerful. They gave people, rather than God, credit for being supernatural. They wanted to offer sacrifices to Paul and Barnabas. Satan is not actually mentioned in this story, but because of the last story we read, we know Satan uses lies and tricks like those we see in this Scripture.*

Satan wants people to think there are many gods, not just one. He wants to distract people from the only true and living God. He knows there is only one God, but if he can make people think there are more gods, he can get their minds off the only true, living God.

Let's look at the differences and similarities between God's powers and Satan's.

Power for What?

(Show the metal container.) I want to show you the power a light bulb has. *(Turn the lamp on. Hold the magnifying glass between the lamp and the container.)* **Will this bulb be able to catch the Kleenex on fire if I magnify the light from it? Why?**

If I did the same thing, only using the sun's power, would the Kleenex catch on fire? *(Demonstrate this by going outside and putting the magnifying glass between rays of the sun and the metal container. Be sure the spot of light magnified is on the Kleenex. It should catch fire quickly. Blow out the flames immediately. If it is overcast, or you cannot catch the rays of the sun, have students tell about times they have used a magnifying glass in this way.)*

If you could choose a source of light and it would be there for a nighttime soccer game, which would you choose—the sun or this light bulb? *The sun. It would give much more light and allow the game to proceed. The light bulb would give only minimal light to the nighttime.*

This experiment can help us see the difference between God's power and Satan's. God is like the sun. Just a tiny bit of His power can do amazing things. Satan is like the light bulb—he has a little power, but his power is not anything like the power of God.

God's power is all about **life**. He shows His power so people can come to Him and get His life. When He heals someone, the healing draws them to Him. They come to know that He loves them. God wants every person to know that He made them, loves them and wants a relationship with them.

5th and 6th graders can become frightened about satanic powers. Reinforce constantly that God's power is more powerful than anything the enemy does. The Scriptures promise He who is in us is greater than the enemy.

Satan's power is all about **destruction.** Satan wants people to be separated from God. He wants to destroy peoples' lives. Jesus said Satan came to steal, kill and destroy.

One way you can tell whose power is at work is that **all power from God will lead people to God**. In the account we read about Elymas, God's power was shown so that Sergius could be lead to God. In the second account, the healing took place so the man healed could be led to God **and** the people around would see God and come to Him.

God's Power for Today

God is more powerful than Satan. God worked His power through people like Paul and Barnabas. What about in our time? Where do we see God's power at work? What about Satan's?

If God's power always leads people **to** God, we can assume that Satan's power always leads people **away from** God. Let's look at some supernatural things we hear about today and see if we can identify where they come from: God or Satan.

◊ **Angels.** Angels are a hot topic right now. Lots of people say that angels have powers, give powers, etc. We know that angels are real. God has revealed them to us in the Scripture. **Is there a difference between biblical angels and the ones we see portrayed on TV shows, movies, etc.?** *Yes. The ones portrayed on television talk about "god," but they are not talking about the God of heaven and earth. These angels do not lead people to Jesus Christ. Jesus said the only way to the Father was through Him. If someone claims you can get to heaven or know God in some other way besides going through Jesus, then they are truly* **against** *God, not for Him. They are leading people in the wrong direction.*

◊ **Crystals.** Many people today believe crystals can help guide and heal them. People have crystals hanging in their homes, from their car mirrors, etc. **Is this wrong?** *It's only wrong if you believe that the crystals can give you power, show direction or bring you closer to God. God does not give any instruction in the Bible about crystals. Instruction from God comes from Him, not from a crystal or any other created thing. True power comes from God, not crystals.*

◊ **Channeling.** This is the New Age practice of allowing a dead person to talk through a live one. This practice is strongly forbidden in Scripture. No one who knows the true living God needs anyone or anything else for direction. God will give direction to all of us.

◊ **Psychics.** These may seem fun or entertaining when you see their commercials on television, but again this practice is strictly forbidden in Scripture. God will tell you everything you need to know about your life when He plans to.

◊ **Ouija boards.** Lots of kids play with this kind of "game." The game supposedly tells fortunes of those playing. The players have to allow the spirits to speak through the game. Again, only God gives Christians directions. This game is satanic. It's a trick to get kids

Nothing or no one is more powerful than God.

involved with Satan. **Have any of your friends or relatives tried to get you to play this game? What could you do if someone does ask you to play?** *Refuse to participate and refuse to stay around while others participate.*

◊ **Spirit-guides.** Some people look to other-worldly beings to show them how to live, what decisions to make, etc. In the New Age movement, "spirit-guides" are promoted to help people in their lives. **Have you seen a TV show or movie or read a book in which a character used an animal or ancestor as a guide?** *(Allow students to respond.)* **Could these be the same as the Holy Spirit?** *No. These guides do not convict of sin. They do not lead people to the true and living God through Jesus Christ. They may say they lead to "god," but it is not the God we serve.* The Holy Spirit is given to us to guide us into truth, to remind us of Jesus' words, to convince us of our sin and to help us pray.

All six of these things are from Satan. They may seem fun or entertaining, but they aren't! They are very real and very harmful! They have been sent to our society, along with many other things, to deceive or lie to us. When people believe in them, they are actually following Satan and his plan for them. The God of the Bible, the only true and living God, has no part in any of them.

Dealing a Death Blow to Satan

Remember that even though Satan is not as powerful as God, he still is very good at what he does—lying to and deceiving people. So, what do you do when you come up against Satan's power? How can you handle it when a friend at school asks you to come over to her house for a seance? How do you as a 5th or 6th grader deal with Satan's power? Let me give you four easy-to-remember steps.

1. **Be with God.** Walk and talk with Him every day. Ask Him for wisdom. He will give you direction, speak to you and give you the wisdom you need every day and every moment. When He lives in you through His Holy Spirit, He gives you discernment. Discernment is knowing what is from God and what is not.

2. **Identify the source of the power.** Remember, all power from God will lead people to God. Trust in your relationship with Him. When you feel that something is not from God, proceed to step 3. If you are unsure, talk with someone you trust, like your parents, Club 56 leaders, children's pastor or pastor.

3. **Listen and obey.** If you have received Jesus Christ as your Savior, He lives inside you. He will give you wisdom and the ability to tell where the power comes from for something. When God tells you something to do, do it.

4. **Watch the results.** Notice what happens when you do what God says. **What happened in the two stories we read this morning?** *Elymas was blinded and the governor believed in God. The man was healed and the people began to see who the true God was.*

Nothing or no one is more powerful than God.

Acts 19:17

All the people in Ephesus, Jews and Greeks, learned about this. They were filled with fear. And the people gave great honor to the Lord Jesus.

Conclusion

Paul and Barnabas walked with God. They went where God wanted them. When Satan's power came against them, they identified the source of power, listened to God, obeyed Him and watched the results of His work.

Remember that God's power is far greater than Satan's. Satan's power is in lying to and deceiving you and others. You can overcome his power by doing the four things we listed: Be with God, identify the source of power, listen and obey, watch the results. God has given you power over the enemy, Satan. You can walk in God's power. Let's pray.

Father God, thank You for Your Holy Spirit who lives in us. Thank You for the wisdom You give us every day. Lord, we need Your wisdom when we deal with Satan. Please help each of us to listen to You in every situation so we can be aware of the lies of the enemy. Help us, Lord, to see what You want to do just as Paul saw that You wanted Sergius to come to know You. We trust You, Lord, to do Your work in us. We are available to listen, obey and watch You work. In Jesus' name, amen.

Materials: Wallpaper samples (or construction paper), permanent markers, pencils, butcher paper, scissors, glue, cardboard and tape.

Before class: From cardboard, cut out four samples each of a triangle, a pentagon (5-sided figure) and an octagon (8-sided figure). All sides of each figure must measure 4 inches in length. Write the Memory Verse across the top of a large sheet of butcher paper. Attach the butcher paper to the wall as the background for the mosaic.

Today's Memory Verse tells us that the people gave honor to the Lord Jesus because of His greatness. You can see our verse on the top of the butcher paper. We are going to make a mural that will display God's awesome power. But first, let's work on memorizing our verse.

Read the verse from the butcher paper and give the students time to memorize it. Then, ask the students to say the verse to three other kids.

We are going to use geometric shapes to create a mural. The shapes from which you can choose include a triangle, a pentagon and an octagon. You will each work with three shapes. They can all be the same shape or they can be different shapes. You will design the shapes to somehow illustrate the power of God. You may choose to use words, symbols or illustrations. When everyone has completed her shapes, we will create a mosaic by putting the shapes on the mural so they all fit together with the sides touching.

The students should use the geometric patterns to trace the shapes onto wallpaper. The shapes should be cut out and designs expressing power made. When all the students have finished, the class will work on fitting together the shapes into a mural. The students may need to rearrange their shapes several times for them to fit together. Then the shapes should be glued in place.

more activities

1—Bible Study

Materials: *Club 56 Activity Zone* page 17, Bibles and pencils.

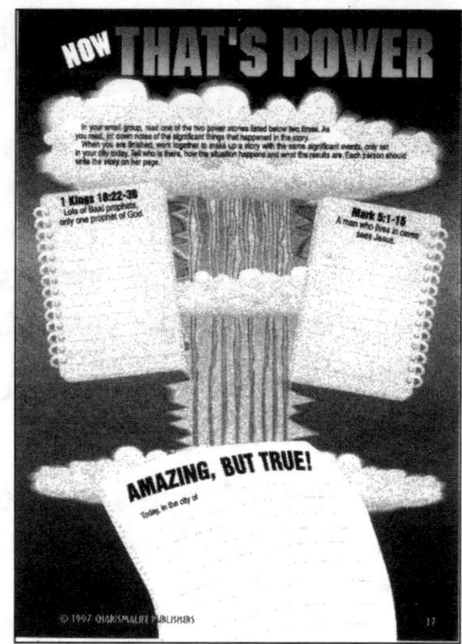

Activity Zone page 17

Who remembers the Power Point today? *Nothing or no one is more powerful than God.* **Let's find some other places in the Bible that show us this truth.**

Hand out the *Activity Zone* page. Have students work for ten minutes in groups of two or three to complete their pages. At the end of ten minutes, call the class back together. Have the groups share the Bible stories they read and the present-day story they made up.

2—Game

Materials: Cotton balls, Vaseline, buckets (two) and wipes.

Divide the students into two teams, and have both teams line up at one end of the classroom. Place the buckets at the opposite end of the classroom.

We learned from our Power Point today that *Nothing or no one is more powerful than God.* Have the first person in each line put a little Vaseline on her fingers and then stick cotton balls onto the fingers.

Look! The cotton balls are "mysteriously" suspended on their fingers! It's a miracle! Let students respond. **There is no mystery or miracle here, of course. The power source is Vaseline. If you didn't know about the Vaseline, it might seem like a mystery, though.**

Now let's see if we can "force the source." Have the first student race-walk to the bucket and then shake her fingers until the cotton balls fall into the bucket. She returns and the next student puts Vaseline on her fingers, races to the bucket and shakes the cotton balls off. Continue until each team member has played.

Have students use wipes at the end of their run to wipe off the Vaseline.

3—Problem Solving

Materials: None.

Are you ever confused as to what is the difference between magic and the supernatural acts of God? Of course, one of the obvious differences is that one serves the good of God while the other's intent is questionable.

Let's look at one specific act that we could compare. Let's look at prophecy and see how a word of knowledge is different from fortune-telling or a so-called psychic's prediction.

Adjust the activities to your class' needs. If you have a small class, do activities with everyone at the same time. If your class is large, break into groups and have each group do a different activity.

Activity Zone page 18

Some of the kids may be unaware that astrology predictions, seances and crystals are of satanic origin. Watch over the productions closely, giving input as necessary. Guide the groups to pray together before deciding how to present their skits. Encourage conversation and interaction after the skits to help students recognize Satan's deceit and defeat in each of the situations.

♦ Name one reason why knowing the future might be good.

♦ How could knowing too much of the future hurt us?

♦ Why might God occasionally reveal what the future holds for us?

♦ Why would God want to restrict us from knowing the future?

♦ How can you tell the difference between something of God and something that is not from God? *God's power always leads people to God and His love for them.*

4—Drama

Materials: *Club 56 Activity Zone* page 18, lunch boxes, newspaper, camera, photographs, pillows and chair.

We've been learning about the power of God today. What is our Power Point? *Nothing or no one is more powerful than God.*

Do you remember the four steps you can take when you must deal with Satan? *1-Be with God. 2-Identify the source of the power. 3-Listen and obey. 4-Watch the results.*

On your *Activity Zone* page there are three situations in which there are two powers at work. You and your group will act out the situation, showing the Christian working through the four steps, which are also listed on the page. Be creative with whichever part you play. You may use any of the props available.

Divide the class into groups of four. Assign situations to groups. If there are more than three groups, make duplicate assignments.

Materials: Copies of Living It Out (story only) and pencils (red).

Hi, I'm Andrew Aaron Westcott. No one in the world has stricter parents than I do! OK, I know I sound a little upset. No, I sound very upset! Do you want to hear this, or are you just going to sit there and stare? I'm sorry, this isn't your fault. Can you take a minute and help me?

I was over at my friend Doug's house last night. He told us he had been playing this really neat game on the Internet. We told him we wanted to see it, so he showed it to us. It was awesome! It was about this battle between good and evil. They had all sorts of players that you can choose, but the most powerful ones are the angels of darkness. They can do anything! Especially when they throw crystals at a challenger. And you choose them by your birth date, kind of like an astrology thing. We played all evening. I didn't even want to stop to eat. It was such a great game, it was like it kept calling me back to play more.

I was so excited that the minute I got home I told my folks about it! Were they happy for me? Oh no. They went ballistic! You should have heard them. I thought they were going to bounce off the walls. Dad would talk and then Mom would take over.

They said Christians shouldn't play games that glorify Satan's power. I tried to explain that it was just an innocent little game. Dad said that nothing Satan does is innocent. He said it's all planned to snare us in his trap of delusion. Now what in the world does that mean?

This is just like my birthday party when Doug got me a Ouija Board. My parents didn't let me keep it! Hey, God can use anything, can't He? My dad said that when you ask the board something you are calling on someone other than God for direction. It's just a little game, people! Why the big deal?

Why are my parents so afraid? I don't get it! Mom says that these games keep wanting you to come back. Well, what's the difference between that and my dad playing Hearts on his computer? Can you tell me that?

Will you talk about this and get back to me? Maybe I'm wrong; I just don't know! Help me, OK?

Can you help?

Divide the class into small groups. Have each group look over the story and find and mark the "red flags"—the statements that identify potential or real problems—that would alert them to trouble.

After they have flagged the statements, have them share with the whole class. End the discussion with the following questions:

- What are the potential dangers of playing games like the ones Andrew was playing?

- Explain why you would or would not play a game like Doug's.

- How can you identify games like Doug's that glorify Satan's power?

- How would you decline an invitation from a friend to play one of these games?

Materials: Copies of *Club 56 Leader's Manual* Lesson 8 ACTS File Page page 99.

Alive Church Technology Services has been asked to design a screen saver for pastors to use on their computers to remind them that nothing or no one is more powerful than God. Your Challenge this week is to design the screen saver. Use the back for ideas you have, other paper to practice on and the computer screen on your file page for your finished screen saver.

Be sure to bring your File Pages back with you next week.

Nothing or no one is more powerful than God.

ALIVE CHURCH TECHNOLOGY SERVICES

Alive Church Technology Services has been asked to design a screen saver for pastors to use on their computers to remind them that nothing or no one is more powerful than God. Your Challenge this week is to design the screen saver. Use the screen above for your design.

ITEMS NEEDED FOR LESSON

☐ ACTS folders
☐ Lesson 8 ACTS File Pages

1—Object Lesson

☐ Construction paper (white and black)
☐ Watercolor paints (red and blue)
☐ Paintbrushes (two)
☐ Food coloring (yellow and blue)
☐ Crayons (red and yellow)
☐ Paper
☐ Newspaper
☐ Bowls (three)
☐ Water
☐ Towel
☐ Pencils
☐ Scissors

☐ Sandpaper (both coarse and fine grain)
☐ Scissors

2—Cooking

☐ *Club 56 Activity Zone* page 19
☐ *Club 56 Leader's Manual* Mayonnaise recipe (page 159)
☐ Salt
☐ Paprika
☐ Vinegar
☐ Lemon juice
☐ Measuring spoons
☐ Measuring cups
☐ Dip mix
☐ Dry mustard
☐ Eggs
☐ Salad oil
☐ Mixing bowl
☐ Electric mixer
☐ Fork
☐ Chips

☐ Bibles
☐ Notebook paper
☐ Pencils
☐ Index cards
☐ Stapler

3—Problem Solving

☐ Chalkboard
☐ Chalk

☐ Bibles
☐ Newspapers

4—Drama

☐ *Club 56 Activity Zone* page 20
☐ Pencils

☐ None

☐ Copies of *Club 56 Leader's Manual* Lesson 9 ACTS File Page page 111

SPECIAL NOTE

Raw eggs, used in More Activities 2, can contain salmonella bacteria, which can cause illness. If you are concerned, use prepared mayonnaise for making and eating the dip.

Conflict: One way to grow.

The apostles and the elders gathered to study this problem. There was a long debate.
Acts 15:6-7a

Acts 11:16-18; 15:5-41; 2 Timothy 4:11

A. Everyone's Invited

B. Separate but Equal

C. Give Peace a Chance

D. Whatcha Gonna Do?

NO MORE ROUGH EDGES

We were in the process of having to repossess a house from a young couple that went to our church. They had abandoned the house to purchase another one. Since we were carrying the contract, the young couple had contacted us and told us to simply tear up the agreement and let them out of the obligation. We were not independently wealthy and were not in a position to be able to afford two house payments. A conflict was born.

We had trusted this couple and had done everything to enable them to buy our house. Now we were being made to look like the "bad guys" when we pushed to enforce the contract they had willingly signed.

Through the kindness and support of a wonderful mediator (who was an attorney from the church), we were finally able to put the conflict behind us. We agreed to release the couple from their obligation and to trust God with the outcome. The final words the lawyer spoke to us were, "Jesus will not let you down."

And He never did. Though we struggled to meet the obligation of two house payments, we never missed one. God constantly surprised us with innovative solutions and miraculous provision. Many times when we thought we would sink, He sustained us.

Conflict is never pleasant, especially when we are in the midst of it. However, I would not trade the changes God produced in our lives through those difficulties. In the fire of adversity we were changed—hopefully to reflect a bit more of our heavenly Father.

If you are in a time of adversity, don't struggle against the change that God is working in your life. Pray that you will be able to accomplish all that He wants to produce in your life. Rest in the assurance that you are in safe hands.

Materials: ACTS folders and Lesson 8 ACTS File Pages.

What was our Power Point last week? *Nothing or no one is more powerful than God.* Your assignment from ACTS was to design a screen saver for pastors to use on their computers to remind them that nothing or no one is more powerful than God.

Let's see your designs. Have each student show his design and tell why it would help remind the pastor of God's power.

Have each student put his File Page in his ACTS folder.

Get involved

Materials: Sandpaper (both coarse and fine grain) and scissors.

Before class: Cut the sandpaper into 2-inch squares. Each student will need two sandpaper squares, one of each kind.

Today we are talking about conflict. What is conflict? *A fight between two people; a difference of opinion; a disagreement; a clash between two different ideas, etc.*

♦ What are some things that might cause conflict in a 5th or 6th grader's life?

♦ Think of one conflict you had this past week. How did you react to it?

♦ Why did you react that way?

Conflict is a part of life. There is no way we can avoid every disagreement with every person. Most of us are uncomfortable when we have to deal with conflict. But what are we so afraid of? Why do we only see it as a negative? Can't conflict have a positive effect?

Hand out two pieces of sandpaper to each student, one coarse and one fine grain. **Look at the pieces of sandpaper I just gave you.**

♦ How do they feel?

♦ What is the job of sandpaper?

♦ Do you think that both pieces do the same job?

♦ What is the difference between them?

Take your pieces of sandpaper and rub them grit sides together. What happens? *The sandpapers smooth each other out, they wear the grit off each other.*

Conflict: One way to grow.

Now rub the sandpaper together as fast as you can. *What do you feel?* *Rubbing the sandpaper quickly together produces friction and thus heat.*

Conflict can be a lot like this sandpaper. When we are involved in a disagreement, sometimes it can rub us raw. It also can produce heat and friction, just as it did when you rubbed the pieces together. Conflict, though, if we allow it, can also smooth away some of the rough spots we may have.

Whether we like it or not, conflict is going to be a part of our lives. The question we are going to explore in our lesson today is not how to avoid conflict but how to properly deal with it. Our Power Point today is *Conflict: One way to grow.*

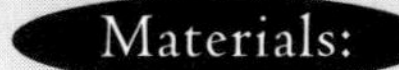 Materials: Bibles, notebook paper, pencils, index cards and stapler.

Everyone's Invited

As the early Church was laying its foundation, there were many difficult decisions it faced. One of these was whether to allow non-Jews (Gentiles) into the Church.

Ever since God had called Abraham to be the father of a new nation, the Jews believed that their race was the chosen one. They had worked at keeping themselves separated from the non-Jews. After living this way for more than 2,000 years, they struggled to accept any non-Jews into their lives. It was a major change and a mind-set difficult to alter.

What finally convinced the early Church was a message from God Himself. He spoke to Peter in a vision and told Peter that His plan of salvation included everyone. *(Read Acts 11:16-18 out loud to the class).*

Now that that hurdle had been overcome, the early leaders were faced with having to decide if the new non-Jewish members had to follow the same ceremonial laws that Jewish believers followed. What should they do? They decided to meet together in Jerusalem and discuss the situation.

Let's turn in our Bibles to find out what happened. Find Acts 15:5-11,19-21. *(Ask for volunteers to read these verses to the rest of the class.)*

♦ How did they resolve the situation? *All sides were allowed to debate the issue.*

♦ Who spoke for the non-Jews?

♦ What was Peter's reason for believing that God had accepted the Gentiles?

♦ How is it that we are all saved?

♦ Do you agree with what was said?

♦ What would have happened to the early Church if a resolution in this matter had not been reached?

Share with the kids how God used conflict to mature you and to help you see His work in your life.

If we turn to Acts 15:30-33, we can read about how the Gentiles reacted to the news. *(Read these verses out loud to the students.)*

It looks as if the early Church, the Church Alive, was able to resolve this disagreement by simply allowing all sides to debate the issues.

◆ Do you think that debating the issues is a good way to solve a conflict?

◆ How does debating an issue help to resolve it?

◆ When, or in what situation, might simply talking about a problem not resolve it?

It is great if we can reach a resolution by simply airing our ideas and calmly talking about them. However, this is only one tool for resolving conflicts both inside and outside the Church Alive. It may not work every time or in every conflict, but it is a good place to start.

Let's look at another way conflict is handled in Acts.

Separate but Equal

Following the resolution of this issue in the early Church, we are told about a disagreement between two of the leaders in the body: Paul and Barnabas.

Turn with me to Acts 15:37-41. *(Ask for volunteers to read these verses out loud while the rest of the students follow in their own Bibles.)*

◆ What were Paul and Barnabas in disagreement about?

◆ Who was right? *The Scripture doesn't say. (Have students discuss who they think was right.)*

◆ How did Paul and Barnabas resolve their disagreement?

◆ Why were they unable to resolve this dispute by simply talking about it?

From what these verses tell us, this conflict between these two leaders was serious enough that it caused Paul and Barnabas to not work together.

◆ Do you think this was an acceptable solution?

◆ Can you think of an instance in your life where you might use this technique?

In a case where there is not a clear-cut scriptural mandate, we have the freedom to follow what we feel in our hearts is the right thing to do.

One way we can double-check our attitudes is by checking to see how we are acting toward the others with whom we have the disagreement. Are we being respectful of their opinions, even though they differ from ours?

Sometimes in conflict there is no right or wrong—both answers would be OK. Remember, it is OK to agree to disagree.

However, the good news is that this is not the end of the story. Turn to 2 Timothy 4:11. *(Read this verse to the class.)*

Wow, does that surprise you? Here is Paul asking for Mark, the very person he thought shouldn't go with them. Not only is he asking for Mark, he is also telling us about how helpful Mark has been to his ministry.

I guess our Power Point is true. Conflict can cause us to grow (and change).

Students will come up against conflicts that they cannot resolve. Encourage them to talk with their parents, you or another trusted adult who can pray for them as they learn to hear God's voice.

Conflict: One way to grow.

♦ How do you think this conflict caused Paul to grow? Barnabas? Mark?

♦ How does conflict bring change and growth in your life?

Give Peace a Chance

We have now looked at two different examples of conflict that Acts gives us. They were resolved in different ways: one through discussion and the other through separation.

♦ Are either of these methods ones which you use?

♦ What are other ways you handle conflict?

♦ Are any of the ways you deal with conflict negative?

OK, maybe some of the ways we deal with conflict are not the best, but, hey, let's be real about this. How in the world are you supposed to discuss things with a younger brother or sister who's really pulling your chain? Or, what happens when your temper gets the better of you? What do you do then?

Let's take a short conflict resolution quiz. It will test some of your attitudes and maybe help you pinpoint some areas you can work on when it comes to conflict. Write a "yes" on the top of your paper and a "no" on the bottom. Put a tally mark under the answer to each question, either "yes" or "no." *(Hand out paper and pencils for the students to record their answers.)*

◊ Do you get mad while trying to resolve conflicts by talking them out?

◊ Do you demand your own way?

◊ Do you think everyone should agree with you?

◊ Does it make you angry when friends don't see things your way?

◊ Do you enjoy conflict?

◊ Do you have a quick temper?

◊ Do you think a person with the opposite point of view is stupid?

◊ Do you think God is always on your side in a conflict?

◊ Do you use sarcastic remarks or put-downs to refer to people who you don't like or who disagree with you?

◊ Do you find it hard to say you are sorry or to admit you are wrong?

Add up the "yes" tally marks on your paper. Scoring: 1-3 yes answers—you're doing great. Keep on the path of peace. 3-7 yes answers—you're doing OK. You need to target some areas for improvement. 7-10 yes answers—yikes!

This little test should help us know where our weaknesses are and what we need to work on so we can deal positively with the conflict that comes into our lives. When we do, we will grow from the difficult situations and come out better at the other end. If we stay stuck in our way of doing things, conflict won't make us better; it will only make us bitter!

Whatcha Gonna Do?

Here is one positive tool you can take home with you this week to help you work on those areas of your life that need to be changed. You are going to make a Scripture booklet that will give you something from God's Word each day that you can make your goal for that day. *(Hand out index cards. Write the following verses on the board for the students to copy, one Scripture verse for each of their index cards. Staple the cards together to form a book.)*

- ◊ Proverbs 17:14
- ◊ Romans 12:18
- ◊ Colossians 3:15
- ◊ Romans 14:19
- ◊ 2 Timothy 2:23-24
- ◊ James 3:17-18

Take your book home with you, and each day read a different Scripture. Pray that throughout the day God will bring the words back to you and help you make your actions line up accordingly.

Conclusion

Conflict is a part of life. There is no way to avoid every disagreement with every person. Thankfully, the book of Acts gives us two ways that help us resolve difficulties that come our way: discussion and separation. When we put these into practice, conflict becomes an opportunity for growth.

Let's pray for His help in resolving conflict. *(Have students get into groups of three or four and pray for each other. Encourage all members to lay hands on one of the members of the group and pray for him. Repeat for each person in the group.)*

Make sure you are applying the points in the lesson to the situations that 5th and 6th graders face. The "Watcha Gonna Do?" section will help you to do that.

Materials: Bibles and newspapers.

We are going to play a game to help us remember our Memory Verses for today. Before we begin the game, I am going to give you one minute to study the verses quietly. You are going to need to know as much of them as you can.

After the minute is up, say the verses together out loud a couple of times. Then have the class sit in a large circle. Choose two students to stand in the middle of the circle. Give these students a section of newspaper. They should roll the sections to make batons.

One of the students in the middle will call out a seated student's name. After saying the name, the person in the middle will run toward the person whose name has been called. The person whose name was called must correctly say the first word of the Memory Verses before the middle person taps him on the head with the newspaper. If the middle person taps him, he must change places with

Acts 15:6-7a

The apostles and the elders gathered to study this problem. There was a long debate.

Conflict: One way to grow.

Have the students write their names on popsicle sticks. Place these in a small container (an old juice can works well). Select a stick from the container when you ask a question, rather than relying on the students to raise their hands. This helps to incorporate more of the students into the discussion.

Remember James 1:19—"always be willing to listen and slow to speak. Do not become angry easily"—as you deal with conflicts in the classroom.

the middle person. If he says the word first, the second person in the middle must quickly call out someone else's name who must then say the second word of the verses before the second middle person taps him. Continue until both verses are said.

Keep the game moving to make it fun and crazy. Play again, beginning with new middle people.

1—Object Lesson

Materials: Construction paper (white and black), scissors, watercolor paints (red and blue), paintbrushes (two), paper, newspaper, bowls (three), food coloring (yellow and blue), water, towel, crayons (red and yellow), paper and pencils.

Before class: Fill two bowls 1/4 full of water. Add yellow food coloring to one bowl of water and blue to the other. The third bowl will be the mixing one.

Today we have been learning about conflict. Our Power Point makes an interesting observation. What is the Power Point? *Conflict: One way to grow.*

Split the class into four groups. Give each group paper, pencils and one of the following sets of materials:

Group 1	Construction paper and scissors
Group 2	Watercolor paints, paintbrushes, paper and newspaper
Group 3	Bowls and towel
Group 4	Crayons and paper

Have Group 2 put newspaper under their work area. Have Group 3 put the towel under theirs.

Have someone in your group keep notes for the group. Each group has two colors that are different. Your group's assignment is to write down the two colors, try to mix them and then write down the changes (if any) you see. Allow groups two minutes to complete this, then bring the groups together. Have each group show their product.

The two colors you all had were conflicting; that is, they were not the same color. Is that correct? Together, though, for some of you, they made a brand new color. When the two colors did combine, they were no longer the color either of them once was. What group had the exception to this? *Construction paper.* Construction paper cannot be mixed with other construction paper to make a new color, can it? It will always be conflicting.

We can be like both the construction paper and the other groups' materials. We are one way on our own—always the same color; yet when we're combined with other people we don't remain the same. We interact with them, resolve conflicts we might have together and become different people.

You should not try to change the way you are for other people, but just as we learned in our Bible Lesson, you should work to resolve conflicts. When you do, the color is beautiful.

2—Cooking

Materials: *Club 56 Activity Zone* page 19, *Club 56 Leader's Manual* Mayonnaise Recipe page 159, salt, dry mustard, paprika, eggs, vinegar, lemon juice, salad oil, measuring spoons, measuring cups, mixing bowl, electric mixer, fork, dip mix and chips.

Note: Raw eggs can carry salmonella bacteria. If eggs cannot be kept chilled, bring store-bought mayonnaise for making the dip.

Conflict can sometimes cause separation. Can you think of any ingredients found in your kitchen that will separate if put together? *Oil and water, oil and vinegar, etc.*

No matter how hard you might shake a jar of oil and vinegar, you won't get them to mix. However, if you add another ingredient, the oil and vinegar will actually mix. The ingredient that allows the two to mix is called an emulsifier.

Hand out the *Activity Zone* pages. **We're going to watch two emulsifiers work in our recipe today. They will allow the oil and vinegar to mix. They are paprika and egg yolk. With these two emulsifiers, we can make mayonnaise.** Make the recipe while the students watch.

Have the students answer the questions on the *Activity Zone* page. When they are done, have them use the fork to add the dip mix to the mayonnaise. While you eat the chips and dip, have students share their answers.

3—Problem Solving

Materials: Chalkboard and chalk.

Sometimes we might think that because we go to church or believe in Jesus we should never have disagreements. In our lesson we heard that even some of the people in the early Church, the Church Alive, sharply disagreed with each other over certain issues. It would be impossible for us to live our whole lives without any conflicts or disagreements.

How we choose to respond in these times is what matters. We can allow disagreements to ruin relationships, or we can choose to work through the problems and grow because of them. Let's brainstorm together to come up with a list of conflicts that might come up between you and your parents, siblings and friends.

Write the conflicts on the chalkboard as the students call them out. If the students are having difficulty, make the following suggestions.

◊ Parents—spending the night at a friend's house, watching certain movies, chores.

◊ Siblings—sharing a room or clothes, using the phone or television.

Activity Zone page 19

Conflict: One way to grow.

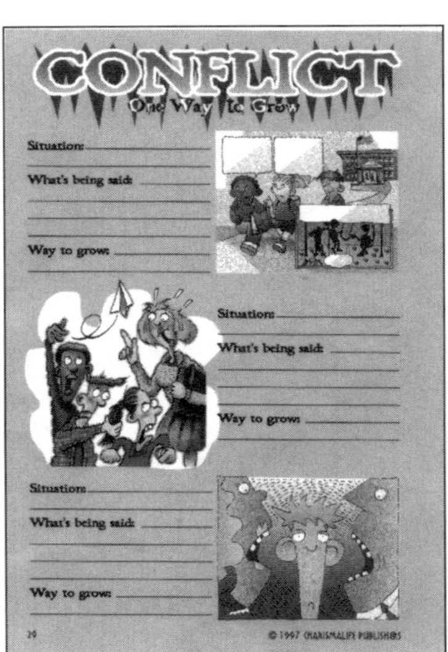
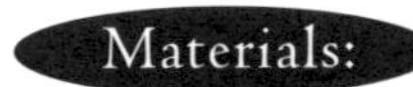

Activity Zone page 20

◊ Friends—jealousy over other friends, doing certain activities.

Have the students work with a partner. Each pair will choose one conflict and discuss two ways of resolving it: one which results in both parties involved feeling good about the decision, and one which results in more conflict and problems.

Give the students four minutes to discuss and resolve the situations. Provide time for the pairs to share their responses with the class.

4—Drama

Materials: *Club 56 Activity Zone* page 20 and pencils.

We all experience conflict. The important thing is to allow it to help us grow in our faith. It can do this if we work toward resolutions to the conflicts we face.

Look at the situations of conflict on the worksheet. Using your imagination, write what the situation is, the dialogue (it's OK to make it funny) and one way for the people involved to grow through this situation.

Be ready to share what you came up with when I call time.

Give students two minutes for each picture. Tell them when each two-minute segment is over.

Have different students share their answers for each picture.

Talia sat in Club 56 with her back to the door. "She really thinks she's something, doesn't she? Dee wants to run everything we do. I think we should raise money for the mission and just give it to them. We could do a bake sale or car wash. This class is supposed to be about all of us!"

Rosa seemed to be looking past her friend to the door. "Rosa, don't you agree with me? Rosa?"

Talia turned to see Dee standing in the doorway listening to their conversation. "Well, I know you heard what I said, Dee, and I'm not going to apologize. Just because your dad is the pastor of the church you think you run everything. This outreach is supposed to be something we all get to decide on."

Dee stared at Talia angrily. "I don't try to run everything, Talia. Is it my fault that I'm usually the one with all the ideas? I don't make people do what I decide. It just seemed like helping at the mission is a good idea. But I don't like hearing you talk about me behind my back! That seems to be something you do all the time, Talia! You're a real gossip!"

Talia's mouth dropped open. "I am not a gossip, and I have plenty of good ideas, too! If you let anyone else get a word in, Miss Kiss Up, you might know that!" Talia jumped up and rushed out of the room.

Dee stood for a minute, then hurriedly left the room. Down the hall, Talia found some of her friends and told them about her disagreement with Dee. She soon had a group of kids very angry with Dee.

Not one to keep her ideas to herself either, Dee found another group and told them what had happened.

By the time Club 56 started that morning, almost the whole class was involved and had chosen sides. Mrs. Prentiss walked into a very angry-looking group.

"My, oh my," she said. "The walls are just rumbling with the sounds of accusations and complaints. It seems like we need to have a problem-solving class today. Does anyone have any ideas on how we might resolve this conflict?"

Each group stared at the other angrily. No one answered.

What would you do?

Ask the class to identify the **real** problems in this conflict. *Each girl wanted her own way. Both formed allegiance groups. Both made it personal.*

♦ What did Talia and Dee want from the class?

♦ How could the class have prevented the conflict from getting out of hand?

♦ What is the earliest point in the story when this conflict could have been settled?

Divide the class into small groups. Have them decide as a group how they would handle this conflict. Then ask each group to share with the class.

Conflict: One way to grow.

Materials: Copies of *Club 56 Teacher's Manual* Lesson 9 ACTS File Page page 111.

Your assignment for the Alive Church Technology Services this week is to observe people in conflict. More than likely you will witness disagreements—even arguments—this week among people in your family, friends at school and other people you hang out with.

Your Challenge is to check out how they handle these situations. Write a one-sentence description for each conflict you witness, leaving out the names of the people involved. For each conflict you record, identify if the people in the conflict responded in good or bad ways. Record your findings on your computer screen.

Be sure to bring your File Pages back with you next week.

Alive Church Technology Services

Check out how people handle conflict. Write a one-sentence description for each conflict you observe this week, then write "yes" if you think the conflict was handled in a good way or "no" if in a bad way. Record your observations on the screen.

ITEMS NEEDED FOR LESSON

❑ ACTS folders
❑ Lesson 9 ACTS File Pages

1—Creative Writing

❑ *Club 56 Activity Zone* page 21
❑ Pencils

2—Group Art

❑ Newspapers
❑ Paint (tempera)
❑ Paintbrushes
❑ Paper
❑ Pencils
❑ Posterboard

❑ Cloth strip

❑ Bibles
❑ Manila envelopes (12)
❑ Roses (four)
❑ Onion
❑ Knife

❑ Feathers (four)
❑ Marker
❑ Tape
❑ Chalkboard
❑ Chalk

3—Game

❑ None

4—Music

❑ *Club 56 Activity Zone* page 22
❑ Bibles
❑ Pencils

❑ Bibles
❑ Construction paper
❑ Markers
❑ Scissors

❑ None

❑ Copies of *Club 56 Leader's Manual* Lesson 10 ACTS File Page page 122

SPECIAL NOTE

Some students may lose interest in the Challenge for the Week. Renew their interest by taking the Challenge yourself, making reminder calls during the week and having your pastor come in to hear what the kids are discovering about the Church Alive.

Not hard of hearing— hard at hearing.

During the night, Paul had a vision. The Lord said to him, "Don't be afraid! Continue talking to people and don't be quiet! I am with you. No one will hurt you because many of my people are in this city."

Acts 18:9-10

Acts 16:9-10; 18:9-10; 20:22-24; 21:10-14; 27:23-25

A. Huh...Are You Talking to Me?

B. But Why Me?

C. Lord, Is It Really You?

HEAVENLY HEARING AIDS

As my bus pulled out of the station, I breathed a heavy sigh—not of relief, but rather of stress and frustration. I had made this trip to a new city to help me make a clear decision as to whether or not I should move. But, instead of making the decision clear for me, it just added new uncertainty.

My head had been throbbing all day. Now, the tension was causing my neck to stiffen. I had to make a decision and make it soon! What was I so worried about? I loved the city. I had a few friends living there, so I wouldn't be lonely. The opportunities for me were endless. So why did I have this unsettling feeling in the pit of my stomach?

Oh, it's just nerves. Once I decide to move, I'll feel great about it, I tried to convince myself.

I was able to reassure myself enough to finally settle in and relax. I could feel an intense exhaustion spreading over me and soon began to doze in my seat.

Suddenly, I woke up with a jolt. My hands were sweaty and my heart was racing. I looked around to see if anyone else had heard what I had just heard. Everyone around me was resting or reading quietly. They obviously knew nothing about what I had just experienced. God had spoken to me while I slept! Although I couldn't remember if I had seen Him, and I couldn't describe His voice, I knew beyond a shadow of a doubt that He had spoken to me. He had given me guidance when I needed Him most.

When I returned home, people asked me why I had decided not to move. As I explained to them the reason for my decision, many of them looked at me as if I were crazy. Still, I knew by the peace in my heart I had heard God's voice. That was all the assurance I needed.

Encourage your students to be sensitive to God's voice this week. He is speaking to them. Are they listening for His call?

Materials: ACTS folders and Lesson 9 ACTS File Pages.

What was our Power Point last week? *Conflict: One way to grow.* **Tell us about the conflicts you observed this week.**

♦ How did the participants handle the situation?

♦ Did the participants respond in good or bad ways?

♦ Which way would you have handled the conflict if you were involved?

Have each student put her File Page in her ACTS folder.

Materials: Cloth strip.

Do you think your hearing is good? Let's see how sharp your listening skills are! We are going to play a game that will let us see just how well some of you can recognize the voices of your friends.

Have one volunteer student go outside the classroom door and blindfold herself using the cloth strip. While she is out, choose three individuals she knows well. When she returns to the room blindfolded, the three individuals are instructed to say a sentence to her, altering their voices in any way they choose. They might make their voices higher or lower or switch to a different dialect. The object of the game is to see if she can identify the voices even though they are disguised.

Give other students an opportunity to be blindfolded. When several students have attempted to identify the disguised voices, discuss the following questions:

♦ **What made it difficult to recognize the voices of your friends?**

♦ **In what ways might God speak to us?** *Through people; in prayer; when we read the Bible; in dreams, etc.*

♦ **Sometimes we might not be sure if it is God's voice we are hearing. How can we know if He is talking to us?**

Get involved

Not hard of hearing—hard at hearing.

Take a few moments to reflect on times when God has spoken to you and be willing to share these openly with your students.

Some students may remain skeptical about God speaking to them. Take some time during the week to pray for your students, asking God to speak to each in a clear and undeniable way.

Materials: Bibles, manila envelopes (12), roses (four), onion, knife, feathers (four), marker, tape, chalkboard and chalk.

Before class: Cut the onion into four pieces. Prepare the manila envelopes as follows: Mark four envelopes "#1" and place a rose in each. Mark four envelopes "#2" and put a piece of onion in each. Mark four envelopes "#3" and place a feather in each. On the chalkboard, make a chart with three columns and three rows. The columns should be titled "Object #," "Characteristics" and "Guess."

Huh...Are You Talking to Me?

Throughout the Bible, we can read about times when God spoke to people. He spoke to them in different ways. Let's turn in our Bibles and find out how God spoke to His people, the Church Alive, in the book of Acts.

(Have students form three groups.) I will assign your group some verses to read. As you read, discover which person heard God speaking and how God spoke to him. *(Allow each group to explain their verses and share their answers.)*

◊ Acts 16:9-10—*Paul, in a vision*

◊ Acts 18:9-10—*Paul, in a vision*

◊ Acts 27:23-25—*Paul, through an angel*

♦ **What do all three of these verses have in common?**

♦ **How did Paul respond when he heard God speak to him in dreams and visions?**

These verses are pretty exciting, aren't they? Paul knew exactly what he should do because God clearly told him. In addition to speaking through dreams and visions, God spoke to the disciples in other ways. In the next passage, we find another way God spoke to Paul. Let's look up the next verse in our Bibles and see how God revealed His message to Paul in this instance.

(Ask for a volunteer to read Acts 21:10-14. Then discuss the following questions.)

♦ **How did God convey His message to Paul?** *Not in a vision, but through someone else.*

♦ **How did Paul respond?**

In the verses we just read, God used another person to deliver His message to Paul. We often call these people "prophets."

♦ **Do you know of anyone in the Bible who was considered to be a prophet?** *Elijah, Elisha, Daniel, etc.*

♦ **Can you name people alive today who would be considered prophets?** *(Students might mention their pastors or other Christian leaders.)*

A third way God spoke to His disciples can also be found in Acts. Choose a partner with whom you can look up Acts 20:22-23. This one may be a little harder to understand than the others, so work together to figure out how God spoke to Paul this time.

(Allow students time to discuss the verse together. Ask for volunteers to share their ideas.) The Holy Spirit was telling him to go; an inner voice speaking to him. God also speaks to us in other ways. **What are some you can think of?** *Through leaders; in the Bible; through other people; through circumstances, etc.*

But Why Me?

Now that we have heard some of the many ways God speaks to people, there is another question we might ask. Why? Why would the all-powerful Creator of the universe bother to speak to people in dreams, through prophets or by impressions? Obviously, He has an incredible love for us if He cares enough to make sure He gets our attention.

There are two reasons why God speaks to His people in Acts. These two will help us understand why He communicates with us. Let's reread a few of the verses we have already seen to find the first reason He spoke to Paul.

◊ Acts 20:22-24

◊ Acts 21:10-11

(Ask for a volunteer to read each group of verses and then discuss the reason God spoke to Paul. The students should come to the conclusion that He was warning Paul.)

♦ **Why would God want to warn Paul about what was going to happen to him?** *To prepare him.*

♦ **What might God warn you about today?**

Besides warning people of things that will happen and preparing them to endure the trials, God also spoke for another reason. Let's look up these verses to find the answer: Acts 27:23-25.

(Have all the students look up the verses and ask for a volunteer to read them aloud.) God wants to encourage us and let us know He will be with us in hard times. He also showed His power to the unsaved on the ship.

Lord, Is It Really You?

(Divide students into four groups. Give each group one set of the three manila envelopes.)

Each group should choose one or two members—examiners—to study the object in envelope #1. Examiners are to close their eyes and examine the object in the envelope to discover its characteristics. They should use all their senses except sight to study the object, then place it back in the envelope. The rest of the group may not give hints or tell what the object is.)

If you examined the object in envelope #1, please describe the characteristics to me. (Have each group's examiner respond. Write her responses on the chart in the appropriate place. Have her guess what the object is.)

(Continue, having groups choose another examiner for each of the other two envelopes.)

Not hard of hearing...hard at hearing.

Be sensitive to students who may fear that a bad dream is a warning from God that something terrible is going to happen. Spend extra time talking about how we can know if it truly is God speaking to us.

♦ Were you able to guess the objects without seeing them?

♦ How did you know it was a rose? an onion? a feather?

We were able to identify the objects because of their characteristics. The same is true about hearing God speak to us. Sometimes we may think we hear Him, but we are not sure if it is really Him. One way we can test the message is to see if it lines up with the characteristics of God.

♦ How could we tell if it lined up with God's characteristics? *(If students leave out certain points, emphasize that the message will agree with the Bible. We can pray. We will have peace, etc.)*

♦ In what ways does God speak to people today? *Dreams, prophets, impressions, the Bible and prayer.*

♦ Has God ever spoken to you? In what ways?

♦ What has God told you when He has spoken to you?

God still speaks to people today. He speaks to each of us in many different ways. But, as our Power Point says, we are not hard **of** hearing, we are hard **at** hearing. In order to recognize His voice, we have to get to know Him. We can do this by spending time with Him, as we do with our other friends.

Conclusion

Just as God spoke to people who were part of the Church Alive in the book of Acts, so He speaks to us today. He could speak to us through dreams, visions, prophets, impressions, the Bible or prayer. God might talk to you to warn, prepare or encourage you. You can know that it truly is His voice if it agrees with His characteristics.

(Give students a few minutes of quiet time to talk to God and listen for His voice.)

Acts 18:9-10

During the night, Paul had a vision. The Lord said to him, "Don't be afraid! Continue talking to people and don't be quiet! I am with you. No one will hurt you because many of my people are in this city."

Materials: Bibles, construction paper, markers and scissors.

Our Memory Verses today are found in Acts 18:9-10. Have students find and read the verses from their Bibles. **How did Paul hear from God in this instance?** *Through a vision of God speaking to him.*

We are learning today about hearing God's voice. **What is our Power Point?** *Not hard of hearing—hard at hearing.* In order for us to remember our theme today, let's write the Memory Verses and Power Point in the shape of something to do with hearing. Use the construction paper, markers and scissors. **What are some things you might draw?** *An ear, a boom box, a hearing aid, a megaphone, stereo speakers, etc.* **You might want to lightly draw the shape first, then write the words around the shape. Be creative.**

Have students share their shapes when they are finished.

1—Creative Writing

Materials: *Club 56 Activity Zone* page 21 and pencils.

In today's lesson, we heard about several ways in which God spoke to people.

♦ What were some of the ways God spoke to the disciples?

♦ Does He still speak to people in those ways?

♦ Has God ever spoken to you in a dream? through another person? by an impression?

God used some pretty dramatic ways to get His disciples' attention. Wouldn't you be amazed if you had a vision in which God told you to move to a new city or a person came to warn you that you would be put in prison for talking about Jesus?

Hand out the *Activity Zone* pages and pencils. Read the directions together and then give the students time to complete the assignments.

2—Group Art

Materials:  Newspapers, paint (tempera), paintbrushes, paper, pencils and posterboards.

Before class:  Cover the tables on which students will paint with newspapers.

God speaks to us in many ways. Why do you think He uses so many ways? *Perhaps so He can get through to each kind of person the way she can hear best.*

We all need help remembering that God speaks to us each and every day if we are listening. To help us in Club 56, we are going to design some posters that we can hang around the room. These are to remind us of all the ways God talks to each of us.

Divide the class into small groups of three or four. Give each group some paper, pencils and posterboard. Assign each group one of the ways that God speaks. Have each group come up with a design on the scrap paper first and then transfer this to the piece of posterboard. Once the design has been sketched, the groups can paint their posters.

When the posters are dry, display them in your classroom.

3—Game

Materials: None.

Today, we talked about listening to God and recognizing His voice. Let's play a game that helps us learn a little more about listening and speaking to Him.

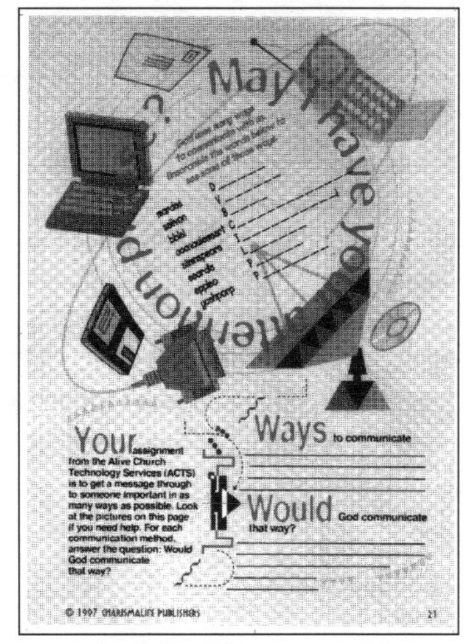

Activity Zone page 21

Answers to scrambled words

mardse	dreams
ssiivon	visions
bblei	Bible
cccnauiemssrt	circumstances
siimnspeors	impressions
eeardls	leaders
eppleo	people
ycehporp	prophecy

Some students may be worried that they will not know if it is truly God speaking to them or just their own imaginations. During class prayer times, vocalize your own uncertainties about hearing His voice and ask God to help you discern when it is Him.

Even the most confident and secure 5th or 6th grader will feel very uncomfortable when the group ignores him during the game. Help students to draw the parallel between how they feel and how others and God feel when we ignore and exclude them.

Not hard of hearing—hard at hearing.

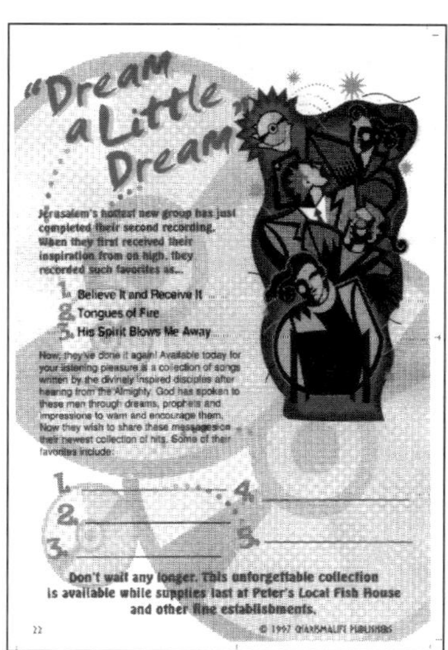

Activity Zone page 22

Ask for three volunteers. These students should leave the room and wait outside for instructions. Give these instructions to the students left in the room.

You should stand around and talk to each other. You can talk about anything you want: school, sports, your friends or what you're planning to do today. When the three volunteers come back into the room, you may not talk with them. No matter what they say, you must completely ignore them.

Instruct the three volunteers that throughout the entire game, their goal is to strike up a conversation with somebody in the group.

Ask the volunteers to come in. Give them two minutes to try to start a conversation with somebody in the group. Then ask them to wait outside again.

Give these instructions to the students inside.

This time, you are all free to talk to the three volunteers, but don't listen to anything they say. Just keep talking if they try to talk to you. You can talk about anything, except what they want to talk about.

Invite the volunteers back in. After two minutes, have everyone sit down to discuss the following questions.

♦ How did it feel to be excluded from the group?

♦ How did it feel to ignore the volunteers?

I think maybe sometimes God feels ignored. He wants to talk to and listen to us, but we're so busy talking to everyone else, we forget He's there just waiting to have a conversation.

♦ How did you feel when you were welcomed into the group and others spoke, but they didn't listen to you?

We do that same thing sometimes with God when we come into His presence and talk and talk, telling Him everything we can think of and asking Him for what we need, but not allowing Him time to talk to us. The next time you spend time with Him, remember to stop and listen to hear what He has to say.

4—Music

Materials: *Club 56 Activity Zone* page 22, Bibles and pencils.

As we heard in today's lesson, God spoke to people in many different ways. We heard how He spoke to His followers through dreams, visions, prophets and impressions. Although this may seem surprising to us, the disciples did not question it. They were sensitive to God's voice and expected to be answered and guided. For this activity, we are going to imagine that we lived during the time of Acts.

Hand out *Activity Zone* pages and pencils. Allow students to work alone or in pairs to come up with song titles that relate to hearing God speak to the disciples. After completing the page, ask students to share their song titles with the class.

"When God gives you a word to share, trust Him that He will make an opportunity." Jesse listened carefully to the evangelist. Usually 5th and 6th graders went to Club 56 during the service, but tonight their leader wanted them to hear the special speaker.

Jesse was glad because lately he thought God was speaking to him. "Does that make sense, Jess?" whispered his dad.

"Kinda, Dad, but how do you know if it's just something you think, or something He's telling you?" His dad motioned for him to listen to the speaker.

When the speaker finished, the pastor invited people to come for prayer. Jesse sat with his dad and watched the prayer teams pray.

"Dad," he whispered loudly, "who is that tall guy over there? Do you know him?"

Jesse's dad looked over and said, "Yes, he's one of the college kids. His name is Bart, and he's a great basketball player. Why?"

Jesse looked at his dad blankly. "Uh, I just wondered, no special reason, really."

But Jesse couldn't keep his eyes off the basketball player. What he hadn't told his dad was that while he was praying he saw a picture of Bart in his mind. Bart was kneeling in front of his bed and seemed very sad. He was saying over and over, "Why me, God? Why me?" Then, Jesse saw someone put His arms around Bart and tell him that he would be OK.

Something inside Jesse kept telling him to go up to Bart and ask to pray for him and tell him what he saw in his mind. But what if it wasn't God? He didn't want to be embarrassed. What if Bart or the other guys with him laughed?

Besides, how could he hear God in his mind sometimes and want to slap his little brother silly the next? It didn't make sense. What should he do? Maybe God would use someone else to tell Bart.

(Divide the class into small groups. Have them discuss the following questions and decide what they would do.)

♦ What was Jesse's greatest concern about telling Bart what he saw?

♦ Jesse was worried that sometimes his mind thought up bad things as well as good. Do you think God will still speak to him?

♦ What do you believe might happen if Jesse doesn't tell Bart?

♦ Would you tell Bart what you believed God is saying?

The end of the story

Jesse told his dad what he believed God had shown him. They prayed together, then went to Bart, Jesse carefully explained the pictures he saw in his mind. When he looked at Bart, he was shocked to see the big athlete crying. "Jesse," he said, "it's true. Will you pray for me?" Jesse took a breath. He'd never prayed out loud before, but he did that night!

Not hard of hearing—hard at hearing.

Not hard of hearing—hard at hearing.

Materials: Copies of *Club 56 Leader's Manual* Lesson 10 ACTS File Page page 122.

The Alive Church Technology Services has asked for your help once again this week. They are doing research on how people hear from God. Your Challenge is to poll a few of your friends, some adults and members of your family about how and what they hear from God. Ask the persons you talk with to explain one way God has spoken to them and what He said. Ask how their experiences affected their lives. Write their responses on the computer screen.

Be sure to bring your File Pages back with you next week.

SUGGESTED SCHEDULE

The following is a suggested time schedule for using *Club 56* in a class time of one hour and 15 minutes. If you have more time, have the class do more of the activities. There is more than enough material from which to choose to build your lesson plans.

MINUTES:

5	Challenge Review
5	Opening Activity
15	Bible Lesson
5	Memory Verse Activity

MINUTES:

25	More Activities
15	Living It Out
5	Challenge for the Week

BIBLE TO USE

We recommend that you use the *International Children's Bible* (ICB) translation of the Scripture. It is easy to understand, is a direct translation and uses words that are familiar to 5th and 6th graders.

In both the *Leader's Manual* and *Activity Zone*, all quotations, Memory Verses and Scripture references are taken from the ICB.

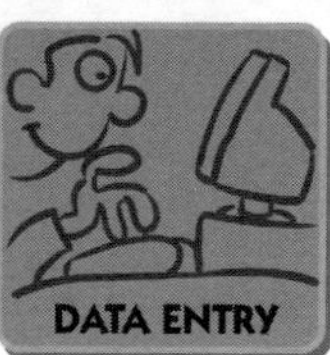

Alive Church Technology Services

Ask around. Find out how people hear from God. Poll a few of your friends, some adults and the members of your family about if and how they hear from God. Ask each person you talk with to explain one way God has spoken to her and what God said. Ask her how this experience affected her life. Write the responses on the computer screen.

Lesson 10 ACTS File Page

ACTS
POWER POINTS

Lesson	**1**	I am part of the Church Alive!
Lesson	**2**	God and people: The real Church.
Lesson	**3**	Walking with God: Never a dull moment.
Lesson	**4**	Know what you believe and believe what you know.
Lesson	**5**	Leadership: Part of God's plan for powerful ministry.
Lesson	**6**	My choices affect many people.
Lesson	**7**	Walking with God: Risky living.
Lesson	**8**	Nothing or no one is more powerful than God.
Lesson	**9**	Conflict: One way to grow.
Lesson	**10**	Not hard of hearing—hard at hearing.
Lesson	**11**	My mission: Anyone, anyplace.
Lesson	**12**	God and I: Ultimate victors.
Lesson	**13**	Acts: The never-ending story.

ITEMS NEEDED FOR LESSON

- ACTS folders
- Lesson 10 ACTS File Pages

1—Individual Art
- Posterboard
- Scissors
- Markers (fine-tip)
- Stamp pads (different colors)
- Hole punch
- Yarn
- Wipes

- Purse (or wallet)
- Play money
- Costumes
- Masks (two, funny)
- Pencil
- Paper

2—Bible Study
- *Club 56 Activity Zone* page 23
- Bible
- Pencils

- Bibles
- Index cards
- Markers
- Chalkboard
- Chalk
- Potting soil
- Oreo cookies
- Cups
- Sunflower seeds (shelled)
- Container (small)
- Water
- Gummy worms
- Plastic spoons

3—Game
- Globes (two)
- Paper
- Pencils

4—Problem Solving
- *Club 56 Activity Zone* page 24
- Colored pencils

- Bibles
- Cassette recorder
- Cassette (blank)

- Copies of Living It Out (story only)
- Paper
- Pencils

- Copies of *Club 56 Leader's Manual* Lesson 11 ACTS File Page page 135

....

SPECIAL NOTE

You will need three adults to participate in a brief skit at the beginning of the class. Read the Opening Activity. Call the volunteers and give them instructions before Sunday morning.

My mission:
Anyone, anyplace.

Then he brought them outside and said, "Men, what must I do to be saved?" They said to him, "Believe in the Lord Jesus and you will be saved— you and all the people in your house."

Acts 16:30-31

Acts 8:26-39;
16:16-34; 17;
1 Corinthians 3:5-7

A. Risky Business

B. Is It Worth It?

C. But It's Just Dirt

D. Risk My Neck?

SPREAD IT AROUND

The emergency room was full when I brought in my daughter. People were milling about, some waiting to see the doctor and others waiting for patients, all of us preoccupied with our own circumstances.

My daughter was bleeding from dog bites. Our neighbor's dog apparently smelled the scent of sheep on her and attacked viciously and without provocation. After verifying insurance coverage at the front desk, I was left to hold and comfort my daughter while waiting for a doctor.

It was several seconds before we understood that the small boy was talking to us. "What happened to you?" he asked. Emilee looked at him, but went back to snuggling rather than answer his question.

I explained that a dog bit her and we were waiting to see the doctor for stitches. His eyes grew big and round. "Did it hurt?"

Now my daughter was forced to answer. "Of course it hurt!" she answered indignantly. "Can't you see I'm crying?" With that, she put her head against my shoulder and glared at the little fellow.

Undaunted, he pursued her further. "Jesus can heal your owies, you know. Have you ever talked to Him before?"

In the pretentious tone of a 5th grader talking to a kindergartner she painstakingly explained that she and Jesus were on very intimate terms. "In fact," she said, "we prayed right after I was hurt." Assuming she had disposed of the little guy, she looked the other way. But he had one more thing to say: "I've known Jesus my whole life, and He's never let me down, not one single time! So if they hurt you in there, you just tell Him about it."

My daughter studied him intently for a minute and then smiled. "Thanks, I will!" she said.

Encourage your class to give witness to their faith this week.

Materials: ACTS folders and Lesson 10 ACTS File Pages.

What was our Power Point last week? *Not hard of hearing—hard at hearing.* **Your assignment from the ACTS was to ask some people how and what they hear from God. What did you find out?** Have students share the information they gleaned this week.

Have the students file their pages in their ACTS folders.

Materials: Purse (or wallet), play money, costumes, masks (two, funny), pencil and paper.

Before class: Ask three adults to participate in a brief skit at the beginning of the class. Have the purse on the table with the play money. Instruct two of the adults to wear costumes and masks and stage a robbery in your classroom by interrupting the class and stealing the purse.

After the robbers leave, go to the door and call for help. The third volunteer will appear. Inspector Harry Hoehangar will enter carrying paper and pencil. He will introduce himself and say that he needs to interview the witnesses to the crime. He will ask them to tell him only what they actually saw. Ask him to occasionally ask the witnesses about something that they would have no way of knowing, like the color of the pastor's tie today. He will interview the students and repeatedly refer to them as witnesses. When his investigation is complete, he should tell the witnesses that he was impressed with their ability to relate the facts.

♦ **How did you qualify as a witness today?** *They saw and heard what happened.*

♦ **Did you answer questions about which you had no knowledge?**

♦ **How did you feel when you didn't know the answer?**

Being a witness is simply telling what we know or what we have seen. Being a witness for God is not difficult when we stick to what we know and believe. Our lesson today is about witnessing to other people about God. The Power Point today is *My mission: Anyone, anyplace.*

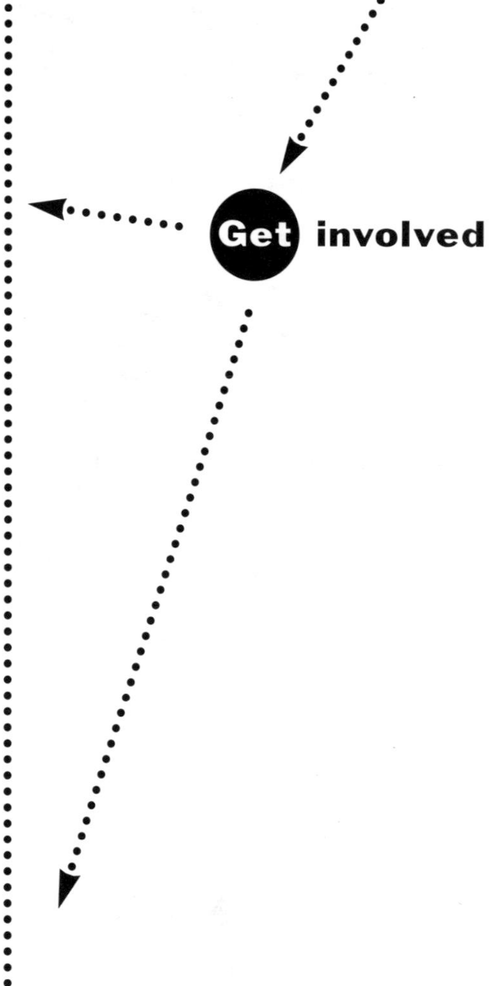

My mission: Anyone, anyplace.

The Power Point should give your entire class time focus. Before class, be sure you can say it from memory. Use it throughout the class time. Have the students repeat it at least once during class, as well as reviewing it next week.

My mission: Anyone, anyplace.

Materials: Bibles, index cards, markers, chalkboard, chalk, potting soil, Oreo cookies, cups, sunflower seeds (shelled), container (small), water, gummy worms and plastic spoons.

Before class: Write the three questions below on each of four index cards. Separate the Oreos and remove as much of the filling as possible from the halves. Put a gummy worm in the bottom of each cup, one per student. Crush the Oreo cookies and fill cups 3/4 full. Put sunflower seeds into one cup. Pour potting soil into one cup. Fill the small container with water.

1. What did Paul and Silas tell the people?
2. Where were they when they witnessed about God?
3. What was the reaction of the people?

Risky Business

What did we learn in that last activity about who a witness is? *A person who tells what he knows or has seen about something.* We're going to learn about some disciples in the Church Alive who were courageous witnesses.

The first part of this story will be familiar to you. We heard about a part of it a few weeks ago when we were learning about risky living. Today we're going to see how that same story shows us Paul and Silas were courageous witnesses of God.

Let's turn to Acts 16 in our Bibles. I need a volunteer to read verses 16 through 21.

♦ **What made the owners of the servant girl mad?** *They couldn't use her to make money anymore.*

♦ **What did they do because of their anger?** *Dragged Paul and Silas to the city rulers, accusing them of making trouble and doing things that were against the law.*

♦ **Were Paul and Silas really making trouble?** *No, they actually helped the girl by commanding the evil spirit to come out of her.*

If you continued reading from there, you would find that the whole crowd joined these owners and were against Paul and Silas. The Roman soldiers tore Paul and Silas' clothes and beat them, then threw them in jail. **Do you think Paul and Silas were wondering if they should have spoken about Christ?** *(Allow students to talk about what their reaction might have been in the same circumstances.)*

Some of you know the rest of this story. God used Paul and Silas to not only free this little girl of a demon, but they also had the opportunity to witness even more. Let's pick up the story again in verse 25. *(Read verses 25-34 aloud as the students follow along in their Bibles.)*

- ◆ **Who else did Paul and Silas witness to?** *The jailer, his family and the prisoners.*

- ◆ **With whom was their witnessing successful?** *The jailer and his family.*

- ◆ **What made the jailer listen to them?** *The earthquake and Paul shouting for him to not kill himself.*

In the midst of a difficult and risky situation, God had Paul and Silas witness to many people. Their witnessing brought salvation to a man and his whole family. If Paul and Silas had run away when the chains fell off and the doors opened, they would have missed the opportunity God had prepared for them.

How might God use difficult circumstances in the life of a 5th or 6th grader as an opening to witness to someone about Him? *(Have students brainstorm ideas of difficult situations they face and how those situations could be an opportunity to share about Jesus. Some difficult situations might be: someone challenges you to a fight; a schoolmate taunts you because you're a Christian; a teacher says your faith is built on fables, etc.)*

Is It Worth It?

Not all witnessing opportunities bring the same results as the one with the jailer. Let's look at some other situations in Acts. *(Divide the class into four groups. Give each group one of the prepared index cards and assign them one of the following to read: Acts 17:1-9, Acts 17:10-15, Acts 17:16-19 and Acts 17:22-34. Each group should be prepared to answer the three questions about their verses. Have each group share their answers with the class. As they share, write the #2 answers on the chalkboard.)*

As we can see *(refer to the list on the chalkboard)*, Paul and Silas didn't stick to one plan or place when they were witnessing. They shared wherever they were. They used many different words to get the attention of people. The results did not always look great.

Paul and Silas were so committed to their responsibility to tell unbelievers about Jesus that they often seemed to ignore circumstances that would have frightened many people. They were willing to be risk-takers. Think about the stories we just read and heard about. **In which of those circumstances would you have been willing to be a risk-taker with Paul and Silas?**

Philip was another believer whom God sent to be a witness. He had been preaching in Samaria when God spoke to him and told him to go to a certain location. *(Have a volunteer read Acts 8:26.)*

- ◆ **What was unusual about God's direction to Philip?** *An angel gave him his orders. He was told to go to a place and simply wait. He had no definite direction other than a location to go to.*

- ◆ **What do you think was going through Philip's mind while he waited for further orders?** *(Have students share what they imagine would have gone through their minds if the same thing happened to them.)*

Philip had to trust God that he was hearing the Spirit correctly. Imagine trusting someone so much that you would do exactly what he said even if it seemed strange. Let's read further and see what occurred in this witnessing opportunity. *(Have a volunteer read verses 27-31 and 35-39.)*

Each of us as believers is asked to share the good news freely with those around us. Ask God to make you sensitive to the kids in your class. Who needs to hear the good news?

♦ **How did Philip witness to the officer?** *He explained the verse of Scripture the man was reading and used it to tell him the good news about Jesus.*

♦ **What were the results of Philip's trust, obedience and witnessing?** *The officer came to know Christ.*

But It's Just Dirt

Sometimes we don't get to see the results of our witnessing. Paul explains this in 1 Corinthians 3:5-7. *(Have a volunteer read the verses.)* **How might these verses help you when you share with someone about Christ?** *Even if the person doesn't pray to receive Christ with you, you can trust that God will send someone else to him.* Your job in witnessing is to listen to God and do what He says. No matter where you are or who's with you, listen to Him and He will give you wisdom in talking to that specific person.

Those verses spoke of planting. They helped us understand that when you plant the truth of God in someone, you can't make that truth take root or grow. It's the same way with actual seeds we plant in dirt. Only God can cause growth.

Maybe you noticed the potting soil, cups and seeds I brought today. Since it's fun to watch things grow, I thought we would plant some seeds today and watch them grow. The soil is already in the cups. Your job is to plant the seeds. *(Hand out the cups with the Oreo crumbs, one to each student. Keep the potting soil cup as yours. Show students how to push the sunflower seeds under the soil by doing so with yours. Pour a little water on your soil, but don't allow the students to add water to theirs.)*

I said earlier that Philip really had to trust God when he went to a place and had no idea what would happen. Now you are going to have an opportunity to trust me. **Do you?** *(Allow students to discuss this while you hand out plastic spoons.)*

I want each of you to eat your potting soil. Go ahead and take a bite; it won't hurt you. *(Don't force them to eat. Normally at least one student will try it and tell everyone else it's OK to eat. If no one volunteers, take one of the Oreo cookie cups yourself and eat a bite of the "soil." Give kids time to eat the treat.)*

Was it easy to trust me? Some of you were willing to do something that seemed strange because you trusted me. When God tells us to go or speak in His name, He will always give us the courage to trust. We just have to reach out to Him and take that courage.

♦ **What was the result of your trust in me?** *You got to eat some sweet stuff.*

♦ **What was the result of Philip's trust?** *Salvation for the Ethiopian man.*

Risk My Neck?

The disciples used many types of witnessing. They talked about Jesus when they were in jail, on street corners, in church and anywhere else possible. Some people get scared about witnessing to other people about Jesus. **What do you think might be scary about witnessing to someone about Jesus?** *You don't know what the person will say. You might get laughed at. You might be rejected, etc.*

What would you say if I told you that witnessing is as easy as breathing? Telling people about Jesus, or witnessing, often happens without speaking a word. How is that possible?

People know a lot about us just from watching how we live. They see how we make decisions and the way we treat others. These observations are part of something we will call "lifestyle" witnessing. People see how you live your life and want to know how you can be peaceful and joyful. They may want to know who gives you courage and strength. **Can you give some examples of people who could benefit from 5th or 6th grade lifestyle witnessing?** *Friends who see you go through injustice without becoming bitter; teachers who notice you are respectful to them; neighbors who see you helping other people, etc.*

Another kind of witnessing involves inviting someone to church, Vacation Bible School, Club 56 or other places where they will hear about Jesus. This kind of witnessing we will call "targeting" because you targeted a certain person, knowing they might be interested in listening and becoming a Christian.

Still another type of witnessing is when someone is having a problem and you tell him how Jesus wants to help him. We'll call this kind "circumstance" witnessing. A certain circumstance in someone's life gave you an opportunity to witness to him about Jesus. **What kind of circumstances might this happen in?** *Sickness, divorce or separation of parents, getting in trouble, etc.*

(Divide the class into three groups. Give them this scenario:

A good friend tells you his parents have decided to get a divorce. He is sad and doesn't know what to do or to whom he can talk. He is asking for your advice.

Have each group take one of the three forms of witnessing and do a short roleplay demonstrating how it might work in this situation.)

Conclusion

A part of being the Church Alive is witnessing to other people what you have seen and heard from God. Witnessing is an exciting and risky **mission** that God has given Christians. It can happen with **anyone** and in **anyplace. As a matter of fact, who remembers our Power Point today?** *My mission: Anyone, anyplace.*

As with Paul and Silas, sharing about Jesus will usually happen as a part of our lives. This week, God will give you opportunities to share Jesus with people you are around. Trust that He will give you the direction and the courage you need. When we pray, ask the Holy Spirit to put someone on your mind to whom you can talk about Jesus this week.

(Pray with the class, asking the Lord to give them the courage and direction to know when and what to share about Jesus. Give them time to pray for the people He puts on their hearts.)

"New Kids' Guide to Sharing Jesus" is available through CharismaLife. It is a new, eight-page tract helping kids understand how to and the importance of witnessing.

A free sample copy is included with this leader's manual.

For additional copies (one for each student), call 1-800-451-4598.

My mission: Anyone, anyplace.

Acts 16:30-31

Then he brought them outside and said, "Men, what must I do to be saved?" They said to him, "Believe in the Lord Jesus and you will be saved—you and all the people in your house."

Thumbprint People

Materials: Bibles, cassette recorder and cassette (blank).

Before class: Ask teachers from adult Sunday School classes if your students can come into their rooms to briefly interview a few students. If your church is smaller and has no adult Sunday School, have students interview adults from the service. Prearrange all interviews.

In our Memory Verses, we hear the jailer ask Paul and Silas what he needed to do to be saved. The man may have expected them to say that he must never sin again or must do many wonderful things before God would consider him worthy enough to be saved, but Paul and Silas had a simple answer for the man. Let's find the verses in our Bibles to see how Paul and Silas responded.

Give students time to look up and read the verses in their Bibles.

When people find out that we believe in Jesus, they may ask us the same question that the jailer asked Paul and Silas. As Christians, how should we respond? Let's find out how other people might answer the question, "What must I do to be saved?"

Divide students into three groups. Before beginning the activity, demonstrate how to operate the tape recorder to record a message. While two of the groups are using their Bibles to memorize the Memory Verses, send the other group into a prearranged classroom to interview some students. Students are to use the question "What must I do to be saved?"

When all three groups have recorded their interviews, play the cassette back for the class. **How did the responses we received compare with the answer of Paul and Silas (which are our Memory Verses today)?**

1—Individual Art

Materials: Posterboard, scissors, markers (fine-tip), stamp pads (different colors), hole punch, yarn and wipes.

Before class: Cut posterboard into 6- by 1 1/2-inch strips. Each student will need one. Make one bookmark as an example. See example of thumbprint people in the column.

It is important for all of us to remember that our mission is to share with anyone in any place God asks us to. To help us remember, we're going to make bookmarks for our Bibles with people figures on them. You will also write the Power Point on the bookmark.

The people you will create are made from your own thumbprint. After the prints are dry you can add hair, feet, hands and faces. Write the Power Point somewhere on the bookmark to help you remember your mission in witnessing to people.

Students roll their thumbs on the stamp pads, then on the bookmarks. They may use the wipes to clean off their thumbs. When they are finished, they can punch a hole in the top and attach a length of yarn to the bookmark.

2—Bible Study

Materials: *Club 56 Activity Zone* page 23, Bible and pencils.

Another person who witnessed about Christ was Ananias. He was reluctant to witness because of the situation he would be drawn into. Let's discover how God prepared and blessed Ananias.

Hand out the *Activity Zone* pages and have the students work alone on them.

When they are finished, ask them to discuss fears that they might have of being obedient to witness. End with prayer for courage and direction.

3—Game

Materials: Globes (two), paper and pencils.

Our Power Point today is *My mission: Anyone, anyplace.* None of us know what place God will ask us to go to witness about Him. We may be like Ananias, who was asked only to go to a certain place in his own hometown. We may be like Paul and Silas—traveling lots of places and telling about Jesus in each place. Or we may be like Philip and be told to go to a road between two cities.

These globes show many countries and continents to which some of us may be called to witness about Jesus.

Divide the class into two teams. Give each team a globe, paper and pencil. One person on each team should be the tabulator of information. We are going to have a relay race of witnessing possibilities. Each of you, on his turn, will spin the globe, let it go around at least two times, then put your finger on the spinning globe and look away. When the globe stops, look at the country on which your finger rests. Tell the tabulator, who will write the country on your team's paper. Then the next person on your team will do the same thing. If a second person's finger is on the same country when the globe stops, the tabulator should make a mark next to that country. If your finger stops on an ocean, the tabulator should mark it as a "Boat Trip." No country is written down and the next person takes his turn.

The point of this game is to get as many different countries on your paper as you can in five minutes. The winning team will be the one with the most different countries.

Call time at five minutes and count the countries.

My mission: Anyone, anyplace.

Activity Zone page 23

Dwight L. Moody, a great man of the kingdom, asked God for the opportunity to share Christ with at least one person each day. Encourage your kids to do the same.

- ◆ **At this point in your life, which countries would you be willing to go to and witness for Christ?** Have students use the lists made by the tabulators or the globes.

- ◆ **Do you think you will be more like Ananias, Paul and Silas or Philip in determining in which places you will witness?**

4—Problem Solving

Materials: *Club 56 Activity Zone* page 24 and colored pencils.

Witnessing comes in a lot of different forms. Can you name some that we talked about today? Allow students to answer.

Sometimes it's difficult to talk to friends about what Jesus has done for you. Imagine that you are afraid to simply tell one of your friends what Jesus has done for you. Instead you get the bright idea to draw a small comic book that will do the talking for you.

Pass out the *Activity Zone* pages. **Use the empty boxes on this page to design a personalized tract that your friend can read. This tract should tell him who Jesus is and how he can get to know and receive Jesus as his Savior.**

After students have finished, invite them to share their tracts with the class.

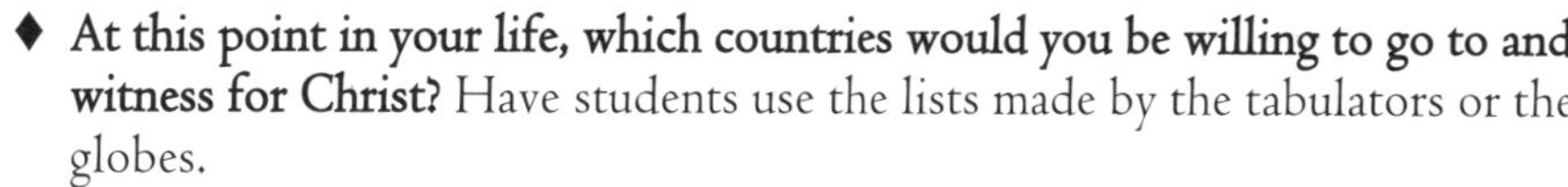

Materials: Copies of Living It Out (story only), paper and pencils.

Hi, I'm MaryBeth Alexander, and I feel like pond scum. I had this perfect opportunity to tell my friend Sally about Jesus, and instead I made her mad. I need someone to listen, OK? Thanks.

Here's what happened. Sally told me the other day that she doesn't go to church. She said that her parents don't believe in God and that she isn't sure about Him either. Well, I decided that I was going to make it my job to convince her about God. Whew! I had no idea how much work it was going to be for me.

I asked my Sunday School teacher for some help, and she gave me a book to read. I wrote down all the Bible verses that might help, and pretty soon I was ready.

Apparently Sally wasn't ready. I invited her over to my house and explained to her that if she didn't ask Jesus to be her Savior she would end up in hell. Sally was a little tense but asked some good questions. She seemed a little ungrateful after all the work I did.

I told her that Christians are happier than other people. We are, aren't we? She was surprised and said that her family was pretty happy, too. I said that was probably because they didn't know any better. Well, that was certainly the wrong

Activity Zone page 24

Students identify strongly with first-person stories. This story is to be read with feeling. It will lose its effectiveness if not presented with excitement and realism. Rehearse it at least three times before class.

thing to say. Sally got up and said that I'm conceited and smug. She stormed out of my house and wouldn't even let me say anything else. And I had so much more to tell her...

You probably know what happened then. Her parents called mine, and now my mom says that I need to apologize. Mom told me that Sally really feels bad about the stuff I said. My own mother says I wasn't very sensitive.

Here I am trying to save her soul, and everyone is mad at me. Does that make sense to you?

I do feel terrible, and now I don't know what to do. Do you think I made a mistake? Where did I go wrong? Will I ever be able to tell her or anyone else about Jesus?

What should MaryBeth do?

Divide the class into small groups. **Give each group a copy of the story. MaryBeth asked a number of questions that need to be answered. Write down the questions that MaryBeth asked and answer them. As a group decide how to help MaryBeth in her relationship with Sally.**

Give groups five minutes to work, then call them back together and have them share the questions, answers and their solutions for restoring the relationship.

Materials: Copies of *Club 56 Leader's Manual* Lesson 11 ACTS File Page page 135.

What is our Power Point today? *My mission: Anyone, anyplace.* **For your Challenge this week, the Alive Church Technology Services (ACTS) has requested your time in inventing a witnessing tool to help Christians tell someone about Jesus. You may invent and design a bumper sticker, button, T-shirt, baseball cap or banner that a person could display to let others know his beliefs. Illustrate your invention on the screen and explain why it would be a perfect witnessing tool.**

Be sure to bring your File Pages back with you next week to add to your ACTS Folders.

Alive Church Technology Services

Alive Church Technology Services has been asked to invent a witnessing tool to help even the most timid Christian tell others about Jesus. You have been asked to participate in this assignment by creating a bumper sticker, button, T-shirt, baseball cap or banner that a person could display to let others know his beliefs. Illustrate your creation on the screen and explain why it would be the perfect witnessing tool.

ITEMS NEEDED FOR LESSON

❏ ACTS folders
❏ Lesson 11 ACTS File Pages

1—Game

❏ *Club 56 Activity Zone* page 26
❏ Pencils
❏ Prizes (two, small)

2—Bible Study

❏ Bibles
❏ Chalkboard
❏ Chalk
❏ Notebook paper
❏ Pencils

❏ None

3—Cooking

❏ Popcorn popper (hot air)
❏ Popcorn
❏ Newsprint (or butcher paper)
❏ Bowl (large)
❏ Napkins
❏ Cups
❏ Juice

❏ Bibles
❏ Dictionary
❏ Chalkboard
❏ Chalk

4—Group Art

❏ *Club 56 Activity Zone* page 25
❏ Bibles
❏ Pencils
❏ Scissors
❏ Tape

❏ Bibles
❏ Cassette player
❏ *Take Me To Your Leader* cassette

❏ None

❏ Copies of *Club 56 Leader's Manual* Lesson 12 ACTS File Page page 147

....

SPECIAL NOTE

In More Activities 3, a hot air popcorn popper is called for. If you are unable to locate one, use the kind with oil. Be sure the students sit far away and do not touch popped kernels for several minutes.

God and I:
Ultimate victors.

We cannot keep quiet. We must speak about what we have seen and heard.

Acts 4:20

Acts 7:54-60; 12:1-5; 16:20-24; Hebrews 10:32-34; 11:24-38

A. Ouch! That Would Hurt

B. Costly Living

C. Do I Have to?

SUFFERING FOR JESUS

He knew if he took a stand he was going to be ridiculed. At the same time, he felt an urging of the Holy Spirit to do the right thing.

His humanities class in college was studying the family. The professor had arranged for a panel of different kinds of family units to visit the class. These included a married couple, a single parent, a live-in couple, a homosexual couple and a communal group. The students were to listen, critique and then present the positive points for each type of family.

With great care and prayer, Tom wrote what he thought Jesus would say regarding each arrangement. As the time came to give his oral report, he envisioned jeers and sneers from his peers. He knew he would be considered a "religious fanatic" by his classmates, but he felt it was time to stand up for the One he loved.

At the end of class, Tom gathered his things and began walking out. The professor stopped him. Tom was ready for his rejection and ridicule. He listened and became confused. Instead of berating Tom, the professor was telling him that in all his years of teaching humanities, he had never had a student stand up for his convictions as Tom had. He had never seen such passion and love for God and people. Although he did not agree with Tom, his heart was touched by Tom's commitment.

What had begun as a great struggle became a quiet victory. Tom was emboldened to share his faith with others. He could not keep quiet.

Materials: ACTS folders and Lesson 11 ACTS File Pages.

What was our Power Point last week? *My mission: Anyone, anyplace.* **Your Challenge was to invent and illustrate a witnessing tool to help Christians tell someone about Jesus. What did you come up with?** After all students have shown their illustrations, have the kids display them on a table or wall. Ask the class the following questions.

♦ Which invention would most likely draw someone's attention to Christ?

♦ Which invention would be the most practical in our city?

♦ Which invention would cost the most?

♦ Which invention would reach the most people?

Have the students file their pages in their ACTS folders.

Get involved

Before class: Make a circle of a few chairs near the center of the room. Put all other chairs around the walls, as far from the circle as possible.

Today in Club 56 we are going to form groups of people who "belong." I will call out a characteristic, and if it includes you, you are in the group—you belong. If not, you will have to stay out. You're unwelcome. For instance, if I say, "Everyone with blue eyes," all the people with blue eyes will sit down together on these chairs. The others will have to sit in the chairs by the walls.

When you're in a group, be excited and talk loudly together about the characteristic and how you like it. Do not talk to anyone outside the group. For instance, if I call the blue-eyed people, you should talk about all the people who love your blue eyes, how blue eyes are better than any other color, how people with other colored eyes just don't belong, how you knew someone with brown eyes once, but you just couldn't be around them anymore, etc.

Are you ready? Here we go. Call one group and give them two or three minutes to talk and exclude everyone else. They should talk loud enough so the "outsiders" will hear. Then change the group by calling the next one.

◊ Everyone who sleeps on a bunk bed.

◊ Everyone with red hair.

God and I: Ultimate victors.

◊ Everyone who is a 5th grader.

◊ Everyone who can recite John 3:16.

◊ Everyone who is home-schooled.

Have the whole class bring their chairs to the center of the room.

♦ How did it feel to be included in the group?

♦ Did you enjoy being outside the group?

♦ What was your favorite group to be a part of?

When one or more people are excluded from a group, and the people in the group harass or taunt them, we can say that the outsiders are suffering. It doesn't feel good to be an outsider.

Today we're going to learn about how the Christians in the book of Acts and others were treated as outsiders. As a matter of fact, they were not only harassed, taunted and made to suffer, they were persecuted just because they believed in Jesus and God and weren't like the other people. Let's get right into the lesson and find out what happened.

Convey to your class the joys of serving Jesus. Don't let this lesson discourage them in their walks. Be strong in sharing the benefits of persecution.

Materials: Bibles, dictionary, chalkboard and chalk.

Ouch! That Would Hurt

What is persecution? *(Have students give their opinions. Let a good reader look up and read the definition from the dictionary. Have students come up with a concise, easy-to-understand definition to use throughout the lesson. One possibility follows.)* Suffering in some way for what you believe, your background or your culture.

Can anyone give me examples of persecution in our world today? *Countries in which civil war rages due to one group's not wanting another to exist; people taunting other people who believe in God; someone blaming someone for something because they are from a certain country, etc.*

Persecution comes in many forms. Whether it is actual bodily harm or taunting someone about their beliefs, it is still persecution. And it hurts. **How have you been persecuted for something?** *(Allow students to answer. Some 5th and 6th graders will tell about times they got in trouble. Be sure to distinguish between true persecution and consequences for bad or poor decision-making.)*

Many people in the past, and even today, have suffered bodily harm and death for standing up for and defending Jesus and the kingdom of God.

Let's check out some examples of people who were persecuted. Two of these passages will be familiar to you because we have looked at other aspects of the situation that is recorded. As you read the examples this time, be ready to tell who was persecuted, why they were persecuted and what the persecution was. *(Divide the class into three groups to read the following verses. Give students about three minutes to work.)*

Acts 7:54-60	Stephen	Jewish leaders were mad at him	Death
Acts 12:1-5	Some who belonged to the church	King Herod wanted to and the Jews liked what he was doing	Terrible things
	James	King Herod wanted to and the Jews liked what he was doing	Death
	Peter	King Herod wanted to and the Jews liked what he was doing	Jail
Acts 16:20-24	Paul and Silas	The owners of the servant girl couldn't use her to make money anymore	Clothes torn, beaten, jail, legs pinned by wood

What did you learn from your verses? *(As students share, make a list of the persecutions on the chalkboard.)*

Wow! There were some pretty bad consequences to sharing about and obeying Jesus, weren't there? Isn't it interesting that these people loved the Lord so much they were willing to suffer for Him? They truly had a hope in Christ that the world could not understand.

What did Stephen see just before he was taken out and stoned? Look in Acts 7:55-56 if you can't remember. *The glory of God and Jesus at God's right side.* God was helping Stephen in the midst of his persecution—God gave him peace and the understanding that God knew what was going on. This must also have made Stephen ready and even excited to go to heaven. As a matter of fact, Stephen was so at peace inside that he prayed for those who were persecuting him. **Can you remember what he prayed?** *That the Lord would forgive the persecutors.*

Costly Living

Hebrews is a book in the Bible that lists people who were full of faith in God and who were persecuted for that faith. The writer includes people even before the Church Alive began. Let's look at what happened to some of these people. Again, find out and be ready to share who was persecuted, why they were persecuted and what the persecution was.

God and I: Ultimate victors.

Ask the Holy Spirit to give you discernment with your class. There may be those who are afraid to serve Christ publicly. Seek His direction for these students and pray for them.

Hebrews 10:32-34	Hebrew Christians	Learned (and apparently lived) the truth	Sufferings, hurt, persecuted before crowds
Hebrews 11:24-27	Moses	Refused to be called the son of the princess	Suffering, anger
Hebrews 11:35-38	Believers in God	Faith in God	Torture, laughed at, beaten, tied up, prison, killed with stones, cut in half, killed with swords, poverty, abuse, bad treatment, had to live in caves and holes in the earth

What did you find? *(As students share, add to your list of persecutions on the chalkboard.)*

These people recognized that walking with God might cost them a great deal, but they knew that they would live with God forever. The victory had already been won for them.

Our Power Point today is ***God and I: Ultimate victors.*** These people and the ones we read about in Acts all realized that ultimately they were victorious because of their relationship with God. The circumstances of the persecution were terrible for many of them, but the assurance of their faith in God and His kingdom made those circumstances bearable to them.

In the first verse of Hebrews 11, there is a definition of our faith. This understanding of faith would help someone endure persecution. *(Read the verse out loud to the class.)* "Faith means being sure of the things we hope for. And faith means knowing that something is real even if we do not see it." **What can we, as Christians, hope for and be sure of, even though we can't see it?** *God, His kingdom, eternal life, heaven, the promises He's made, etc.*

Do I Have to?

We have read now about severe kinds of persecutions that happened to people who followed God. Some of the persecutions, though, didn't involve bodily harm or death. Look at the list and tell me what other kinds of persecutions there were. *Suffering, anger, laughter, poverty, bad treatment, terrible things, jail, clothes torn. (As students reply, underline these persecutions on the chalkboard.)*

Most likely, none of us have suffered persecutions of bodily harm, and of course, none of us have suffered death for our faith. We will, though, suffer some of these other kinds of persecution because we believe in God and Jesus Christ.

♦ **Can you share an experience of persecution you have had that had one of the underlined consequences?**

♦ **Have you stood up for what is right and been made fun of for doing so?** *(Give them a chance to share the experiences they have had. Be sure to encourage them for having done what is right.)*

Whenever possible, have students look up and read Scripture from their own Bibles. This helps them become familiar with their copy of it.

♦ For what or whom would you be willing to suffer?

There will be times in your class at school, with your friends or in your neighborhood when you will need to stand up and speak for God. For instance, a teacher might challenge your beliefs or your friends might dare you to do something wrong to be included in their group. Will you be willing to risk laughter? bad treatment? suffering?

What was it that the people from the Bible did to help them through the persecution? *They remembered that they were already victorious, regardless of the cost to their bodies, because of their relationships with God.* God has won the ultimate victory in our lives. He has defeated death through the sacrifice of Jesus Christ. Death can't defeat you or me.

♦ **If you live and are persecuted, who will help you?** *Jesus.*

♦ **If you die because of persecution, where will you go?** *To heaven to be with God forever.*

Our Power Point is absolutely true: **God and I: Ultimate victors.** Although we may be mistreated, made fun of and ridiculed for believing in and trusting God, the victory is ours through Christ!

Conclusion

Persecution is not easy to take. It doesn't feel good. We have learned, though, that God has already won the victory on our behalf. He will be with us through any persecution we face.

There will continue to be persecution in the world against those who walk with God because people who don't walk with Him are directed by Satan, who wants to persecute God's people. As Christians, though, we know that persecution is only temporary. We can rejoice in the victory that God has provided for us both here and in heaven.

Let's pray now and ask God to give us His strength when we face persecution.

(Close with a prayer of thanksgiving for the opportunity to suffer for Christ and the privilege of having His strength in facing persecutions. Ask the Lord to give each student the strength she needs this week when facing opposition.)

Share times when you or someone you know was persecuted for her faith. Your class needs to know there are people today standing up for their faith.

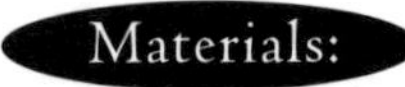
Materials: Bibles, cassette player and *Take Me To Your Leader* cassette.

Before class: Cue cassette to "God Is Not a Secret to Be Kept."

Acts 4:20

We cannot keep quiet. We must speak about what we have seen and heard.

God and I: Ultimate victors.

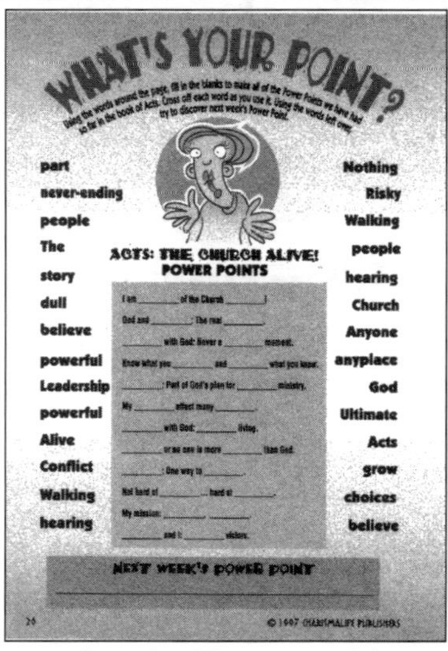

Activity Zone page 26

Take Me To Your Leader is a recording by the Newsboys. If you do not own a copy of the recording, check with students in your class, teenagers at the church or your local Christian bookstore for a copy.

Our Memory Verse is from early in the book of Acts. The Jewish leaders had put Peter and John in jail for preaching about Jesus. The next day, the leaders told Peter and John not to speak or teach at all in the name of Jesus. Our Memory Verse is Peter and John's response to the leaders. Have students find the verse in their Bibles and say it with you.

♦ What is it that Peter and John could not keep quiet about?

♦ What might they face because they took this stand? *Persecution.*

Peter and John did face persecution because they continued to live by what they had said. You also can live by this verse. You might face some persecution, but you will be sharing God with others who do not yet know Him.

One way to share what we know is through music. Maybe you have heard of a popular Christian group called Newsboys. Listen with me to one of their songs, "God Is Not a Secret to Be Kept."

♦ In what way does this song help you to remember our Memory Verse?

♦ Is there a phrase or part of the words that stands out to you?

♦ How might sharing this song with a friend be a good way to witness?

♦ What kind of persecution might the Newsboys encounter because of their beliefs?

1—Game

Club 56 Activity Zone page 26, pencils and prizes (two, small).

Answers can be found on *Club 56 Leader's Manual* page 123.

We've been studying the book of Acts now for 12 weeks. That means we have learned 12 different Power Points. Using the *Activity Zone* page I will give you in a minute, try to write all of the Power Points we have had. There are specific directions on the page which you must follow. The first person done with the 12 correctly written will receive a prize. The first person who guesses next week's Power Point correctly will also get a prize. Before I give you the page, let's say today's Power Point together. *God and I: Ultimate victors.* That will give you a start.

Pass out the *Activity Zone* pages and pencils. Have students work alone. Give the first person with all 12 done correctly one of the prizes. Give the other prize to the first person to correctly guess next week's Power Point.

2—Bible Study

Materials: Bibles, chalkboard, chalk, notebook paper and pencils.

Before class: Write the following references on the chalkboard.

- ◊ Matthew 5:10-12
- ◊ John 15:18-19
- ◊ Romans 8:18
- ◊ 2 Corinthians 4:8-9
- ◊ 2 Corinthians 12:10
- ◊ 2 Timothy 3:11-12
- ◊ Hebrews 12:3
- ◊ 1 Peter 2:19
- ◊ 1 Peter 4:14
- ◊ 1 Peter 4:16
- ◊ 1 Peter 5:10

Look up at least five of the verses I have listed on the chalkboard. Find out what some Bible writers experienced, thought or wrote about suffering for Christ. On your papers, write the encouragement offered about suffering for Christ.

When everyone is finished, have someone share about each verse listed. **Which of these verses might help you when you are persecuted for what you believe? Write the reference on your paper and circle it. Put the paper in your Bible and anytime this week when you are mistreated or teased about following God, find and read the verse from your Bible. The Holy Spirit will encourage you with the words of that verse.**

3—Cooking

Materials: Popcorn popper (hot air), popcorn, newsprint (or butcher paper), bowl (large), napkins, cups and juice.

Spread newsprint out on the floor. Set the popcorn popper in the middle of the newspaper. Display the popcorn seeds for the students to see. **How does this little seed turn into popcorn? What causes it to pop?** *Heat causes the seed to explode.*

Pour several seeds into the popper. Leave the lid off the popper and allow the popcorn to pop out of the popper and onto the newspaper.

The popcorn seeds become so filled with heat that they cannot contain themselves any longer and have to explode. Peter and John felt the same way when they were told to stop speaking about Jesus. They were so filled with the Holy Spirit that they could not contain their excitement. They wanted everyone to know. The relationship they had with Jesus "popped out." They could not help speaking about what they had seen and heard.

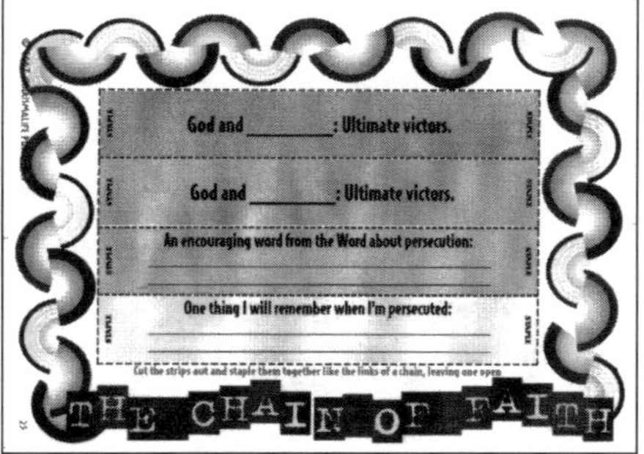

Activity Zone page 25

Pour more seeds into the popper with the lid in place. Place a bowl under the spout. Pop popcorn for the students to enjoy. Also, provide cups of juice for the students to drink.

4—Group Art

 **Materials:** *Club 56 Activity Zone* page 25, Bibles, pencils, scissors and tape.

We have been blessed because of the persecution of the Christians before us. We enjoy religious freedom in our country and in many other countries in the world today because of the stands taken by Christians who lived at other times.

We're going to make a Chain of Faith today, helping us realize that those who were persecuted before are a part of who we are today. Think of people whom you have read about, know or have heard about today who have been persecuted for Christ.

Give students their *Activity Zone* pages. They should follow the instructions, filling in the names of Bible characters or other historical figures who were persecuted for their faith, as well as their own names, Scripture verses about persecution and something they will remember when they are persecuted.

When the class is finished, link the chains and hang them on the walls around the room.

"Bruce, you can't really believe that, can you?" asked his teacher, Mrs. Larsen. "People don't sin, Bruce. They make mistakes."

The kids laughed, and Mrs. Larsen continued to talk. "If you make judgments about people like that, you're setting yourself up for trouble."

Bruce had answered a question the teacher asked about World War II. Now his face was bright red, and he had no idea what Mrs. Larsen was saying. *Why did I answer that question?*

"So, Brucey, you gonna save all the sinners around here?" taunted Jim. He and his friends surrounded Bruce during recess. "I kinda thought you were the preacher type."

"Leave me alone, Jim," answered Bruce. He pushed his way past the boys and went back into the school.

After school that day, the boys found him again. "On your way to church, Bruce?" laughed Jim. As Bruce passed him, Jim shoved him up against the chain-link fence. "People like you think you know more than anyone else. My aunt acts just like you. My dad says she's haywire and thinks God actually talks to her. What a laugh!"

Bruce cleared his throat nervously. "God does talk to people, Jim..."

Before the words were even out of his mouth Jim had knocked him into the fence again. "What a dummy!"

Turning to the crowd of kids that were gathering, he spoke tauntingly. "Bruce says that God comes down from heaven and has little chats with him. Does God come and talk to you, Paul? Rick? No? That's too bad. Can we give you a message to send to God for us, Bruce?" The kids were laughing uncontrollably.

"What's going on here, people?" It was the principal, Mr. Drake.

Jim answered, "Nothing, we're just talking to Bruce. Isn't that right, Bruce?"

Everyone turned and looked at Bruce. Mr. Drake smiled at him. "Bruce, are you OK?"

Now what am I going to do? he wondered. *These people already think I'm a jerk! What will they do if I say anything more? But why should I let them treat me like this? Maybe Jim needs to get into trouble!*

"Bruce," said Mr. Drake insistently, "what's going on?"

What do you think Bruce should do?

Before any discussion, ask the class to vote on what they would do: keep quiet or tell Mr. Drake about the persecution.

Divide the class into two groups on the basis of how they voted. Assign each group to prepare a defense of their position. (If the vote was very uneven, divide the class in half and assign each group one position to defend.) Have the groups present their positions. When they have finished their presentation, ask them the following questions:

♦ How does your defense measure up with the Bible Lesson today?

♦ Is your defense honest?

♦ Would your defense work in "real life"?

♦ Would you personally use this decision and defense?

God and I: Ultimate victors.

Materials: Copies of *Club 56 Leader's Manual* Lesson 12 ACTS File Page page 147.

When people become Christians, they sometimes make the mistake of thinking that their new lives will be totally easy and carefree. They are surprised when something goes wrong or they are actually persecuted for their beliefs.

Suffering because of being a Christian builds character and strengthens our relationship with the Lord. Your Challenge for this week is to think of three people whom you admire because of their relationships with the Lord. Ask them about persecution they have faced in their lives. After you've done your research, write about their experiences on the computer screen.

Be sure to bring your ACTS File Pages back with you next week.

Alive Church Technology Services

Talk to three people whom you think of as strong Christians. Ask them to tell you about experiences when they were persecuted because of their Christian beliefs. Ask them to share what they learned, how the experience affected their relationship with the Lord and if they have any regrets.

ITEMS NEEDED FOR LESSON

- ❏ ACTS folders
- ❏ Lesson 12 ACTS File Pages

1—Game

- ❏ Chalkboard
- ❏ Chalk (two pieces)
- ❏ Bubble gum

2—Drama

- ❏ *Club 56 Activity Zone* page 28
- ❏ Microphone
- ❏ Props (such as robes or shawls)

- ❏ Copy of *Club 56 Leader's Manual* page 123
- ❏ Bell

3—Creative Writing

- ❏ Paper
- ❏ Pencils

- ❏ *Club 56 Activity Zone* page 27
- ❏ Bibles
- ❏ Pencils

4—Problem Solving

- ❏ Index cards
- ❏ Marker
- ❏ Bowl (or paper bag)

- ❏ Bibles
- ❏ Towels (four)
- ❏ Plastic bottles (four, 20-ounce soda bottles work well)
- ❏ Teaspoons (four)
- ❏ Measuring cups (four, 1/4 cup)
- ❏ Vinegar
- ❏ Baking soda

- ❏ None

- ❏ Copies of *Club 56 Leader's Manual* ACTS File Page page 158

SPECIAL NOTE

Reviews of what we've learned are great teaching tools. Use today's review of Acts to help solidify the teachings from the past 12 weeks.

Acts: The never-ending story.

He preached about the kingdom of God and taught about the Lord Jesus Christ. He was very bold, and no one tried to stop him from speaking.

Acts 28:31

Acts 8:1-24; 9:1-22; 10:9-48; 19:11-20; 23:11-24

A. Don't Miss This
B. The Church Continued
C. The Church Continues

IT NEVER ENDS

It was a simple game fashioned from a single sheet of notebook paper. This was then folded into squares and triangles that could be held on the tips of your fingers. Carefully written under the folds of paper were such valuable pieces of information as who you would marry, how many kids you would have and what your favorite color was.

Though the answers always changed, we seldom grew tired of this guessing game. Much of our recess time was filled with playing it. We all had a high level of interest in where our lives were going—even if we were only 12 and there was only the smallest chance that the information would be even remotely correct.

(As I remember, one of the many predictions given to me was that I would have 11 children, marry Kevin Hudson, and love the color red—none of which proved to be accurate.)

Our lives can't be predicted. Only God knows what is contained in my life's book. Each day, however, God gives us the privilege of a new blank page. Following His direction, it is ours to fill. As you walk through this week, think about what that page has to say about you. What kinds of events and activities are you allowing to fill up your page?

Your 5th and 6th grade students also need to be reminded about how their lives speak for them. As you wrap up the study of Acts this week, both you and the students must grasp that the next chapter to write is yours. What will the pages say about each of you?

Materials: ACTS folders and Lesson 12 ACTS File Pages.

What was our Power Point last week? *God and I: Ultimate victors.* We looked pretty closely at persecution. The ACTS company sent us on a mission to each find three people whom we admire in the Lord and find out what persecution they've encountered in their lives.

Please share your findings with the class. Have each student share his information.

♦ Did any one of the people surprise you in his response? If so, how?

♦ How did talking with these people help you in facing the prospect of persecution in your life?

♦ Were you persecuted this week for believing in Jesus? If so, how?

Materials: Copy of *Club 56 Leader's Manual* page 123 and bell.

Before class: Divide each Power Point into two parts by drawing a slash through the middle of the statement. For example, Lesson 1 would be "I am part/of the Church Alive." Place enough chairs for each student in two straight rows, each chair facing forward, one in front of the other. Place the bell on a table about 5 feet from the front chairs of the teams.

We have come to the end of our study of the book of Acts. Acts records the beginnings of the early Church and ends with the approaching death of Paul, one of its main leaders. However, the story of the Church doesn't end at the book of Acts. It continues on and new chapters are added all the time. How could this be? *It's a record of the acts of people who received Jesus Christ as their Savior and followed God. We are those same kinds of people, so although our books won't go in the Bible, we are continuing to "write" the chapters with our lives.*

Since this is our last lesson, let's play a review game to remind us of some of the Power Points we have covered. We did a review of these last week with our *Activity Zone* pages, so you should be great at it this week.

Divide the class into two teams. Have each team sit on the chairs, one in each row.

I will give you one half of one of the Power Points—either the beginning or the ending. In order to receive a point for your team you must supply the other half.

Acts: The never-ending story.

Read half of the Power Point. When the front person from either team knows the answer, he must run to the table and ring the bell. Award his team a point if he answers correctly. If he doesn't, then allow the first person on the other team to try.

The first person on each team then moves to the back chair and everyone on the team moves up one chair.

Go through all the Power Points, alternating between reading the beginning and ending of different ones. Count up the points at the end to declare the winning team.

The Power Points are one way of reminding us about the history of the Church. Let's begin our lesson and continue on with the "never-ending story."

Materials: *Club 56 Activity Zone page 27, Bibles and pencils.*

Don't Miss This

The book of Acts is the second book which Luke wrote. It tells us what happened to the early Church after Jesus' death and resurrection. Without Acts, think of all the important events we've learned about that we would have missed. **What are some of those events?** *(Have students share what they can remember.)*

I am going to break you into groups and have each group do some research in Acts. We have covered lots of stories and events from the book, but we didn't cover everything. Your group's job is to read and be ready to tell the highlights of the verses I give you. All of these are significant stories that we have not looked at.

(Break the class into five groups. Assign each group one of the following as their topic to research.)

◊ Acts 8:1-3, 9:1-9,17-22 — Conversion of Paul

◊ Acts 10:9-16,34-35,44-48 — Peter's vision from God

◊ Acts 8:5-13,17-24 — Simon tries to buy the Holy Spirit

◊ Acts 19:11-20 — Sons of Sceva learn they need to know Jesus to use His name

◊ Acts 23:11-24 — A plan against Paul is foiled

As you are researching, consider these questions: What happened? Why might this event be important? How did this event help the Church grow?

(Allow the groups five minutes to do the research. At the end of the time call the groups back together and have them share the information they have found.)

In order for the small groups to be productive, assign a student leader to help keep each group on task.

All of these events were important happenings in the early Church, as were the ones we've studied these past 12 weeks. Without Luke recording them for us, we would have missed all this valuable information. Acts gives us an historic look into the formation of the Church Alive.

The Church Continued

One of the exciting things about reading and studying the book of Acts is that the accounts given were only the **beginning** of the Church Alive. We were introduced to many great leaders in the early Church, but it doesn't stop there. In the almost 2,000 years since, there have been many other great people who have inspired and led the Church. Let me tell you just a few things about some of them. When I say their names, raise your hand if you've heard of them.

◊ John Wycliffe (1330-84). English philosopher, theologian and religious reformer. He believed in a direct relationship with God for each believer, without the need for a priest between the two. He translated the Bible from its Latin form into English so it could be read by anyone.

◊ Martin Luther (1483-1546). German theologian and reformer. He initiated the Protestant Reformation, which led to the breaking away from the many traditions of the Catholic Church.

◊ John Calvin (1509-64). French theologian, pastor and church reformer. He believed and taught that every word of the Bible was absolutely true. He also encouraged people to believe that everything that happens in the world was decided by God before anything existed. He pointed all believers to the Word of God as their source of truth. He also urged the Church to remain pure and to not keep doing sins.

◊ Sojourner Truth (1797-1883). Her birth name was Isabella. She was a slave until 1827, when she was emancipated. She had a dramatic salvation experience and began to evangelize, sharing with others the good news. She traveled and preached throughout the New England states.

◊ William Booth (1829-1912). English leader and founder of the Salvation Army. The Salvation Army provided (and still provides) spiritual help and food, clothes and other practical things to the needy.

◊ Aimee Semple McPherson (1890-1944). Evangelist and faith healer. She rallied many denominations to work together for the kingdom of God. She held tent meetings and revivals throughout the United States and Canada, with tens of thousands of people being saved. Began the first radio station in the city of Los Angeles. It was dedicated to declaring the truth of God's Word.

◊ Kathryn Kuhlman (1907-76). Evangelist and faith healer. She held revivals throughout the United States. She was instrumental in beginning the use of radio and TV to declare the gospel to people.

◊ Billy Graham (1918-   ). American evangelist. He taught the Bible to large audiences through tent revivals before using television as a way to reach a large number of people with the gospel. He still preaches about God in large stadiums around the world.

These are just a few of the people who helped to continue writing the book of Acts. They accomplished many great things just as the early leaders did.

Acts: The never-ending story.

Boldness comes in many different forms. Pray that God's boldness rests on each of your kids as they face a variety of situations this year.

The Church Continues

So now, here we are—Club 56 on Sunday morning. **How do you and I continue the book of Acts?** *(Have students give suggestions of how this might happen through their lives or yours.)*

Those were good ideas. One way to continue the book of Acts in our day is for each of us to write down our experiences of walking with God. I will make it easy for you to start by giving you an information sheet to fill out. *(Hand out the Activity Zone page to each student. Allow students time to fill them out before regrouping and sharing their stories with each other.)*

Just as the book of Acts records the events of the early Church, your own book can record the events of your life, which is part of the Church Alive today.

Conclusion

The growth of the early Church is recorded in the book of Acts. It is the story of God's redeeming power through Christ and the coming of His Spirit to live in and work through each believer. That story did not stop at the end of Acts. The story has continued to be written, though not always on paper, through the lives of those who have given themselves to God and His kingdom.

The story is being written today by you and me as we follow God and do the things He asks us to. We continue to be the Church Alive. Our Power Point says it very well: *Acts: The never-ending story.* Let's pray that we will continue to be the Church Alive all of our lives and that we will be part of God's never-ending story.

Father, we love You. We're so glad that we have had all these great examples in men and women who have lived before us and followed You with their whole beings. We also want to be the Church Alive today, God. Please help us by reminding us to listen to Your Spirit. We will choose to follow Him when He speaks to us. Lord, when each student in this class is grown up, please continue to remind him that he is invited to be part of both the Church Alive and the never-ending story.

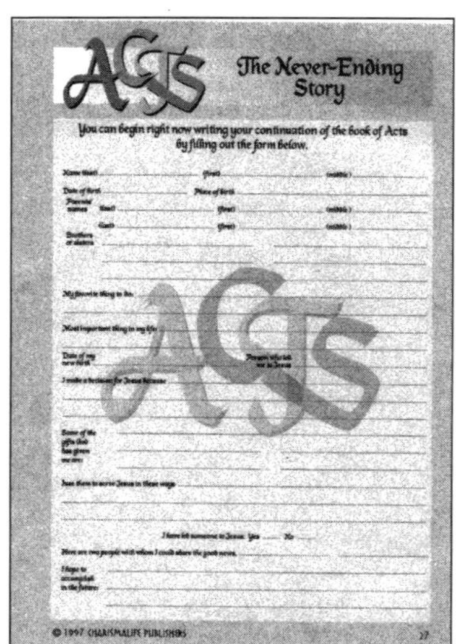

Activity Zone page 27

Acts 28:31

He preached about the kingdom of God and taught about the Lord Jesus Christ. He was very bold, and no one tried to stop him from speaking.

Materials: Bibles, towels (four), plastic bottles (four, 20-ounce soda bottles work well), teaspoons (four), measuring cups (four, 1/4 cup), vinegar and baking soda.

At the end of the book of Acts, the very last verse says this about Paul: "He preached about the kingdom of God and taught about the Lord Jesus Christ. He was very bold, and no one tried to stop him from speaking." This is a great conclusion! Through all the trouble he and others went through to share the gospel, here it says that no one tried to stop him from speaking anymore. He had freedom to share his faith.

As you memorize this verse, think about being bold yourself and having no one try to stop you from talking about God. When you're finished, we're going to do an experiment that illustrates why Paul and many others in the book of Acts continued telling about God, even when they were persecuted. Give students about three minutes to memorize the verse.

Set out the vinegar and baking soda on a table. As you can see, we have two common ingredients that you probably have at your house. Alone, neither one does anything. However, when the two ingredients are mixed together, they cause a reaction to take place. Let's find out what happens when the two mix.

Divide the students into four groups. Give each group a towel, a plastic bottle and a spoon. Ask students to spread out the towel and place the plastic bottle in the center of the towel. Then, pass around a bottle of vinegar and a measuring cup. Instruct each group to measure 1/4 cup of vinegar and pour it into the plastic bottle.

Next, circulate a box of baking soda and ask each group to fill their teaspoon with baking soda. Ask the students to hold the spoons until given further directions. When all of the groups are ready, ask them to add the baking soda simultaneously. The vinegar and baking soda will bubble and foam until it spills over. The towels should absorb all of the overflow. The reaction only lasts a few seconds.

When the reactions have stopped, discuss the following questions with the students:

♦ What happened when you added baking soda to the vinegar?

♦ When the bubbles popped, what was released into the air? *A gas.*

♦ Could the bubbles and gas remain in the bottle? *No, they spilled over.*

♦ How long did the reaction last?

Just as the vinegar and baking soda forcefully overflowed when they were combined, so it was with people in the early Church when they were filled with the Holy Spirit. They had such a deep relationship with Jesus that their love for Him spilled over.

The same can happen to each of us when we are close to Jesus. But just like the vinegar and baking soda, the reaction will last only a short time unless we continually keep alive our relationship with Him. We need to be the Church Alive every day by listening to the Holy Spirit and doing what He says.

Acts: The never-ending story.

God has called each of your kids to serve Him in a specific way. Each one has been given gifts to fulfill God's calling. Ask God to help you develop and encourage those gifts within each one.

1—Game

Materials: Chalkboard, chalk (two pieces) and bubble gum.

We've learned a lot in our study of Acts. Let's see how well you can recall the stories and Power Points.

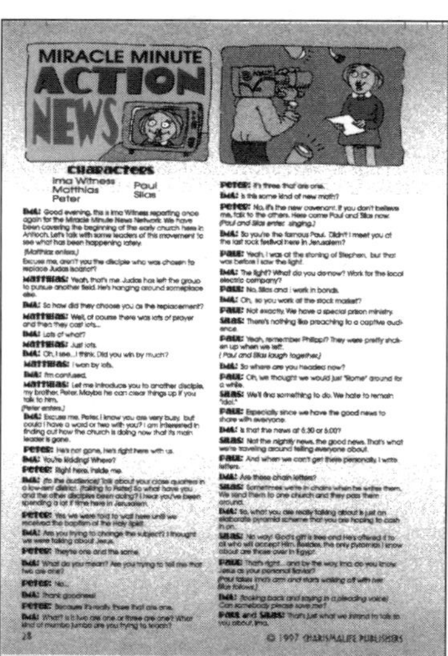

Activity Zone page 28

Allowing students to share their finished work helps build confidence and self-respect. Be strong in having the rest of the class be a respectful audience.

Split the class into two teams. Give the first person on each team a piece of chalk. The first person on both teams will go to the chalkboard to draw. Using your leader's manual, whisper in their ears one of the stories or Power Points of the past 12 weeks' lessons from the book of Acts.

On your signal, both kids will begin drawing something to remind their team of the story or Power Point. The team members will shout out the story or Power Point they think is depicted. When someone gets it right, that team gets a point and the next kids from both teams come to the board to draw.

Continue until all team members have had a chance to draw. Award the winning team a piece of bubble gum for each team member.

2—Drama

Materials: *Club 56 Activity Zone* page 28, microphone and props (such as robes or shawls).

Have students get into groups of five. Give them the *Activity Zone* page and have them practice the skit. Give the groups props and have them perform for the class.

3—Creative Writing

Materials: Paper and pencils.

Now that we have finished the story of Acts, we're going to do some creative writing to share what we remember.

Do you know what a limerick is? It is a five-line poem that has a specific form. In the five lines of your limerick, lines 1, 2 and 5 all need to rhyme and contain seven syllables. Lines 3 and 4 rhyme and have only five syllables. Here is an example of one:

> There once was a man named Paul
> Who preached the gospel to all
> He took not a cent
> Wherever he went
> But was faithful to his call.

Use your imagination and let's see what you can come up with from all that you have learned from Acts.

Have students work individually or in pairs. When they are finished, have them share their limericks with the class. Make this a fun and light time.

4—Problem Solving

Materials: Index cards, marker and bowl (or paper bag).

Before class: Write the following questions on individual index cards. Place these in the bowl.

Note: The lesson that could apply, as well as the Power Point from that lesson, are given in italic for the leader's reference only.

◊ What would you say if your friend is a Christian, but thinks that the only time he has to act like one is at church on Sundays? *Lesson 2. God and people: The real Church.*

◊ What would you say if one of your friends called the psychic network and now two of the predictions that she was given have come true? *Lesson 8. Nothing or no one is more powerful than God.*

◊ What would you say if a Christian friend tells you he's really not that excited about God and church and he is wondering why it seems so dull? *Lesson 3. Walking with God: Never a dull moment.*

◊ What would you say if you are really mad at your best friend. She won't listen to your opinion, and you need to convince her to see things your way? *Lesson 9. Conflict: One way to grow.*

◊ What would you say if your friend has been a Christian for most of his life, but still doesn't feel comfortable sharing what he believes with others? *Lesson 11. My mission: Anyone, anyplace.*

◊ What would you say if you had a hard time accepting that Jesus is the only way to be saved? *Lesson 4. Know what you believe and believe what you know.*

◊ What would you say if you were asked to help serve on an inner-city ministry team? *Lesson 11. My mission: Anyone, anyplace.*

◊ What would you say if your best friend just accepted Jesus and is asking you a lot of questions for which you're unsure of the answers? *Lesson 4. Know what you believe and believe what you know.*

We have learned many important things by studying the book of Acts. Let's put that knowledge to work for us by figuring out the answers to some of these tough problems. As you read these, think about the Power Points and parts of the lessons we've studied.

Have one student at a time draw out an index card and read the situation to the class. Have the entire class try to reach a solution based on the information they have learned from previous lessons.

Liza watched her grandmother limp slowly toward the kitchen. She hoped she would get a snack and go back to her room before the kids got there. Grandma could be so embarrassing sometimes. No one could understand her because of that accent, and she was always going on with stories about God and the old country.

"Grandma Kate, I'll carry your snack to your room." Her grandmother smiled, and Liza felt guilty. "I love you, Grandma."

"Thank you, child. I love you, too. God has blessed me over and over with the wonderful heritage of grandchildren." She hugged Liza, but instead of going to her room she went into the family room and sat down.

If your class is larger than eight students, form teams to answer each situation.

Find time during class to quietly talk with each student, encouraging him to be part of the Church Alive today and in this next week. Pray with him for this to happen.

"Grandma, some of the kids are coming over tonight to plan our Sunday School outing. We might be too loud for you," she said hopefully. "Wouldn't you like to listen to the radio in your room?"

"Liza," her mother called, "May I see you in the sewing room for a minute, please?" That wasn't a tone that Liza liked to hear.

"I have a feeling," said her mother when they were alone, "that you're trying to get Grandma out of the family room. Am I right?"

Liza sighed deeply, "Oh Mom, you don't understand. Grandma is wonderful, but she tells too many stories. Please don't be mad at me!"

"I'm not mad, honey. Grandma and Grandpa deserve our respect for many reasons. They endured many horrors in concentration camps in Holland. They trusted God, and He brought them through. Grandma Kate loves to tell the stories because they are her tribute to God. She's a treasure, Liza. Maybe if **you** were positive and enthusiastic about Grandma with your friends they would respect her. I think they sense your embarrassment and don't know how they should act around her. Nevertheless, you will treat your Grandmother respectfully. Do you understand?" Liza looked down and nodded. "Liza, Grandma has given us a wonderful heritage of faith. Don't forget that."

Her mother just didn't understand. She heard the kids coming up the front steps.

What should Liza do?

Discuss the following questions with the whole class.

♦ What purpose do Grandma Kate's stories serve?

♦ How could Liza help her grandmother share her stories?

♦ How is remembering your heritage important?

♦ What is your spiritual heritage?

Divide the class into small groups. Have them decide how Liza should handle her predicament.

Acts: The never-ending story.

Copies of *Club 56 Leader's Manual* Lesson 13 ACTS File Page page 158 and ACTS folders.

Your Challenge this week is to analyze the Challenges from the past 12 weeks and develop three recommendations you would make to our pastor to help our church continue to be the Church Alive. The recommendations may be programs to start, sermons to teach, activities to continue, things you will be doing differently in your life, etc. You make the call.

Be sure the students have their File Pages and folders.

Invite the pastor to visit your class next week so the class can present their recommendations.

ALIVE CHURCH TECHNOLOGY SERVICES

What have you learned about our church as a consultant for Alive Church Technology Services? What part do you think our church will play in the future of God's Church? Your Challenge this week is to analyze the Challenges in your ACTS folders from the past 12 weeks and develop three recommendations you would make to our pastor to help our church continue to be the Church Alive. The recommendations may be programs to start, sermons to teach, activities to continue, etc. You make the call.

ACTS RECIPES

Before beginning either of the following recipes with the kids, please be sure to follow these guidelines:

◊ Teachers and students should wash their hands thoroughly with soap and water before cooking.

◊ At no time should students be left alone in the room to work on any of the cooking projects. Always have at least one adult present.

Warning: Cooking can be dangerous if students begin getting silly, throwing ingredients, etc. If someone begins to get silly while cooking or preparing to cook, make it clear that her privilege of helping with the project will be revoked if she doesn't stop immediately. Follow through with your promise if she continues and have her sit out during the activity.

Lesson 2

Play Dough

- ❑ 1 cup flour
- ❑ 2 teaspoons cream of tartar
- ❑ 1 tablespoon cooking oil
- ❑ 1/2 cup salt
- ❑ 1 cup water
- ❑ Food coloring

Put all ingredients in a saucepan and cook, stirring constantly until mixture forms a ball and pulls away from pan. Knead on a flour-covered surface until cool. Store in an airtight container.

Lesson 9

Mayonnaise

- ❑ 1 teaspoon salt
- ❑ 1/2 teaspoon dry mustard
- ❑ 1/4 teaspoon paprika
- ❑ 2 egg yolks
- ❑ 2 tablespoons vinegar
- ❑ 2 cups salad oil
- ❑ 2 tablespoons lemon juice

Mix dry ingredients. Blend egg yolks into dry ingredients. Add vinegar and mix well. Add 1/4 cup salad oil, 1 teaspoon at a time while beating with an electric mixer. Slowly add 1 1/4 cups oil. Mix well. With the last 1/2 cup of oil, add a little oil, then a little lemon juice, mixing well after each until all oil and lemon juice are in the bowl. Makes 2 cups mayonnaise.

ACTIVITIES CHART

ACTS: The Church Alive!

Each activity brings home the Power Point, Memory Verse or one emphasis of the Bible Lesson.

m = Memory Verse Activity *w = Worksheet Activity* *r = Reproducible Page*

Week	Drama	Music	Creative Writing	Bible Study	Individ. Art	Group Art	Object Lesson	Cooking	Game	Problem Solving	Outreach Project	Research	Discussion
1		✓		✓(w)	✓(m)				✓	✓(w)		✓(r)	✓
2	✓(w)					✓(m)	✓		✓(w)		✓	✓(r)	✓
3			✓(w)		✓			✓(m)	✓	✓(w)		✓(r)	✓
4				✓(w)		✓(w)	✓		✓(m)	✓		✓(r)	✓
5				✓(w)	✓			✓	✓(m)		✓(w)	✓(r)	✓
6		✓(w)	✓(w)			✓(m)			✓	✓		✓(r)	✓
7		✓			✓(w)		✓(m)		✓(w)		✓	✓(r)	✓
8	✓(w)			✓(w)		✓(m)			✓	✓		✓(r)	✓
9	✓(w)						✓	✓(w)	✓(m)	✓		✓(r)	✓
10		✓(w)	✓(w)		✓(m)	✓			✓			✓(r)	✓
11				✓(w)	✓		✓(m)		✓	✓(w)		✓(r)	✓
12		✓(m)		✓		✓(w)		✓	✓(w)			✓(r)	✓
13	✓(w)		✓				✓(m)		✓	✓		✓(r)	✓

ACTS MEMORY VERSES

Lesson 1	Acts 1:8	But the Holy Spirit will come to you. Then you will receive power. You will be my witnesses—in Jerusalem, in all of Judea, in Samaria, and in every part of the world.
Lesson 2	Acts 2:42	They spent their time learning the apostles' teaching. And they continued to share, break bread, and to pray together.
Lesson 3	Acts 3:16	It was the power of Jesus that made this crippled man well. This happened because we trusted in the power of Jesus. You can see this man, and you know him. He was made completely well because of trust in Jesus. You all saw it happen!
Lesson 4	Acts 4:12	Jesus is the only One who can save people. His name is the only power in the world that has been given to save people. And we must be saved through him!
Lesson 5	Acts 6:3-4	So, brothers, choose seven of your own men. They must be men who are good. They must be full of wisdom and full of the Spirit. We will put them in charge of this work. Then we can use all our time to pray and to teach the word of God.
Lesson 6	Acts 7:60-8:1	He fell on his knees and cried in a loud voice, "Lord, do not hold this sin against them!" After Stephen said this, he died. Saul agreed that the killing of Stephen was a good thing.
Lesson 7	Acts 13:2	They were all worshiping the Lord and giving up eating. The Holy Spirit said to them, "Give Barnabas and Saul to me to do a special work. I have chosen them for it."
Lesson 8	Acts 19:17	All the people in Ephesus, Jews and Greeks, learned about this. They were filled with fear. And the people gave great honor to the Lord Jesus.
Lesson 9	Acts 5:6-7a	The apostles and the elders gathered to study this problem. There was a long debate.
Lesson 10	Acts 18:9-10	During the night, Paul had a vision. The Lord said to him, "Don't be afraid! Continue talking to people and don't be quiet! I am with you. No one will hurt you because many of my people are in this city."
Lesson 11	Acts 16:30-31	Then he brought them outside and said, "Men, what must I do to be saved?" They said to him, "Believe in the Lord Jesus and you will be saved—you and all the people in your house."
Lesson 12	Acts 4:20	We cannot keep quiet. We must speak about what we have seen and heard.
Lesson 13	Acts 28:31	He preached about the kingdom of God and taught about the Lord Jesus Christ. He was very bold, and no one tried to stop him from speaking.